Senegal

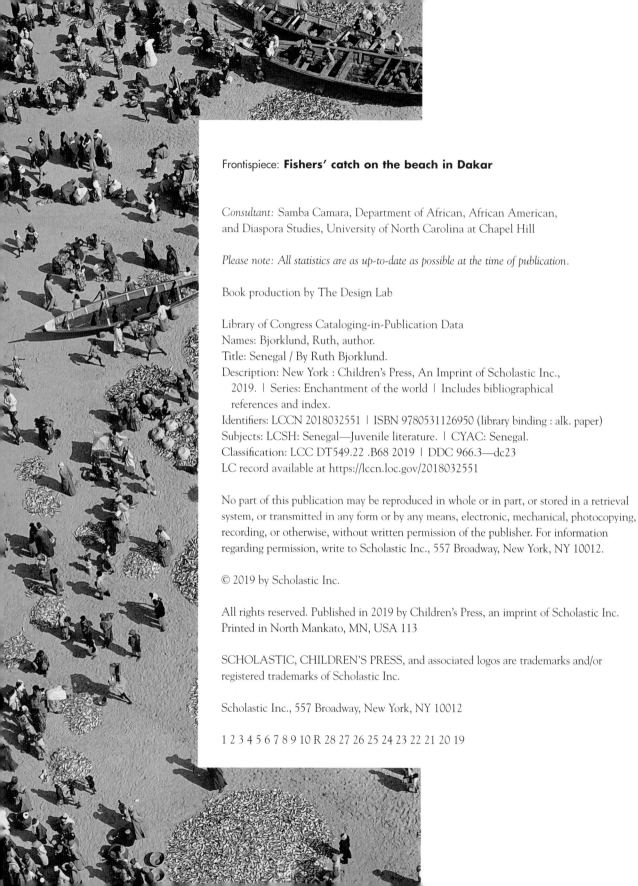

Frontispiece: **Fishers' catch on the beach in Dakar**

Consultant: Samba Camara, Department of African, African American, and Diaspora Studies, University of North Carolina at Chapel Hill

Please note: All statistics are as up-to-date as possible at the time of publication.

Book production by The Design Lab

Library of Congress Cataloging-in-Publication Data
Names: Bjorklund, Ruth, author.
Title: Senegal / By Ruth Bjorklund.
Description: New York : Children's Press, An Imprint of Scholastic Inc.,
  2019. | Series: Enchantment of the world | Includes bibliographical
  references and index.
Identifiers: LCCN 2018032551 | ISBN 9780531126950 (library binding : alk. paper)
Subjects: LCSH: Senegal—Juvenile literature. | CYAC: Senegal.
Classification: LCC DT549.22 .B68 2019 | DDC 966.3—dc23
LC record available at https://lccn.loc.gov/2018032551

All rights reserved. Published in 2019 by Children's Press, an imprint of Scholastic Inc.
Printed in North Mankato, MN, USA 113

SCHOLASTIC, CHILDREN'S PRESS, and associated logos are trademarks and/or registered trademarks of Scholastic Inc.

Scholastic Inc., 557 Broadway, New York, NY 10012

1 2 3 4 5 6 7 8 9 10 R 28 27 26 25 24 23 22 21 20 19

Senegal

BY RUTH BJORKLUND

Enchantment of the World™
Second Series

CHILDREN'S PRESS®

An Imprint of Scholastic Inc.

Contents

Left to right: **Grinding palm nuts, red-throated bee-eaters, Lac Rose, bus, jewelry**

CHAPTER I

Friends and Family

April 4 is coming soon, and Mariama is very excited. April 4 is Independence Day, the day that Senegal gained independence from France. While Mariama is proud of her country and happy to celebrate the holiday, she is even happier to spend time with her parents' families. Schools close for two weeks in Senegal to celebrate Independence Day, and Mariama's parents always travel to visit friends and family.

For the first week of their vacation, they will visit her mother's family in Saint-Louis, about 125 miles (200 kilometers) north of their home in Thiès. On their way back, they will stop for a visit with her father's family in a small village not far from home.

Thiès is a pretty city not far from the capital city of Dakar. Mariama's father works in the mayor's office. Many people in

Opposite: **Senegal is a young country. More than four out of every ten Senegalese are less than fifteen years old.**

KEY
⊛ Capital
● Major city
○ City
■ National park

MAURITANIA

Djoudj National Bird Sanctuary

Dagana ○Bokhol

Kaédi

Saint-Louis○

EUROPE   ASIA
Area of map

AFRICA

○Louga

Matam○

Lompoul○

○Linguère

Ferlo Desert National Wildlife Preserve

Pikine ○Touba

Bakel○

Dakar⊛ ○Thiès

○Rufisque

SENEGAL

Mbour○ ○Diourbel

○Fatick

MALI

●Kaolack

○Kaffrine

Saloum Delta N.P.

○Koungheul

ATLANTIC OCEAN

○Tambacounda

THE GAMBIA

CASAMANCE

○Vélingara

Niokolo-Koba N.P.

○Bignona ○Kolda

Ziguinchor○

Népen○ ○Kédougou
Diakha

N
W E
S

Basse Casamance N.P.

0   80 MI
0   80 KM

GUINEA-BISSAU

GUINEA

their family work in the government, as do many other members of Senegal's largest ethnic group, the Wolof. The Wolof people are Muslims, as are most Senegalese. In some ethnic groups, like the Wolof, women and girls over thirteen can own land. Unlike in some Muslim countries, Muslim communities in Senegal do not require women to cover themselves with a traditional robe or veil. Instead, women wear colorful headscarves and wraps and Western-style skirts and dresses. Both men and women wear *boubous*, long cotton robes.

Mariama's family will take a *sept-place* (meaning "seven seats" in French) taxi to Saint-Louis. Her family does not own a car. The streets in Thiès are crowded. There are many buses and taxis, trucks, cars, and bicycles, and in some neighborhoods, horse and donkey carts. Mariama's house is not far from schools or the marketplace, so it is easy to walk where they want to go. Her father rides a motorcycle to work. Thiès is a bustling hub of activity. It is a major marketplace for farmers

In Senegal, buses are often brightly colored. People sometimes stand on the bumper of the crowded buses when there are no seats available.

In the semiarid
grasslands of northern
Senegal, many people
are herders.

and livestock herders from all over the region. There are many factories, including a famous one that makes tapestries designed by Senegalese artists.

The Drive

The sept-place takes Mariama and her family through a changing countryside. Outside of Thiès, where her father's family lives, are tens of thousands of acres of peanut farms. The area is called the peanut basin. Senegal is a major exporter of peanuts around the world. Beyond the farms, grasslands stretch as far as anyone can see. The Fulbe people live in the area. They are cattle and goat herders. Mariama loves the large jewelry the women wear.

They turn west and take the coastal road north. They plan to spend the night at Lompoul. The Lompoul Desert, with its large sand dunes, is wild and beautiful. Mariama would one day like to see eastern Senegal, especially Niokolo-Koba National Park. It is very remote and one of the last places where West African wildlife such as lions, savanna elephants, and baboons live.

After climbing the dunes at Lompoul and enjoying the ocean breezes, Mariama's family goes to a restaurant for her father's favorite dish, *thieboudienne*, the national dish of Senegal. It is a thick, spicy casserole made of stuffed fish, tomato sauce, hot peppers, vegetables, tamarind, and hibiscus flowers. It is served over rice in a big bowl that everyone shares.

The next day, Mariama's family continues on to Saint-Louis. Once the capital of all the French colonies in West Africa, it has many tree-lined streets and historic buildings. They arrive around lunchtime. The family skipped breakfast that morning, knowing their relatives would overwhelm them with food and treat them like royalty. This is *teranga,* the Senegalese way. *Teranga* means "hospitality." Senegalese people value sharing and caring above all else.

The days together in Saint-Louis are spent eating and talking under the large, shady eucalyptus tree in the family compound. Mariama loves to listen to her father and his brothers-in-law and friends talk and tease each other.

One day, the family has a fun trip planned. They will go to the Langue de Barbarie peninsula. The word *langue* means "tongue" in French. The peninsula is a long, thin sandy stretch of land along the coastline, separating Saint-Louis from the open ocean. Saint-Louis is an island in the mouth of the Senegal River. This time of year, millions of migrating birds, such as terns, swans, and herons, make their nests in the dunes and swamps along the peninsula. Sea turtles also nest in the sand. Mariama and her brothers and cousins stay on the beaches of the east side. The Atlantic Ocean on the west side is too rough for swimming. On their way home, Mariama's family stops at a small fishing village. Mariama watches as hundreds of small motorboats and pirogues (wooden canoes) unload their catch.

Heading Home

At the end of the week, Mariama and her family hire another sept-place to return south. Before they arrive home in Thiès, they stop to visit her father's family. His three brothers no longer live in the family's village. They had worked on a peanut plantation. But many peanut farms have gone through hard times. Worldwide demand for peanuts and peanut oil has decreased. Also, the land itself is not as productive as it once was. Farmers have overworked the soil, and there have been several droughts. So, Mariama's uncles have left the village and immigrated to France to work and send money home.

With her uncles away, the gathering is much smaller. Her grandmother, two aunts, and four cousins greet Mariama and her family with a great deal of teranga. After chatting under the shade of an immense baobab tree, they take a walk out of town to see her grandmother's garden. Most Wolof people have a piece of land to farm. Mariama's grandmother farms not only her own plot but those of her sons who live in France. Her garden is bursting with vegetables and fruit trees. She is proud that she grows enough food to feed her family with more left over to sell in the market.

On the drive back to Thiès, everyone is quiet. They are sad to leave family behind. But school will begin again in a few days, and Mariama and her brothers look forward to once again playing and joking with their friends. Even back home, they will enjoy the warmth and teranga of Senegalese culture.

Senegalese relax on the beach in Dakar.

CHAPTER 2

A Place in the Sun

JUTTING OUT INTO THE ATLANTIC OCEAN, SENEGAL IS continental Africa's westernmost country. The country is a mix of dry desert lands, vast grasslands, and wet rain forests. Lakes sprinkle the landscape, and four major rivers cross Senegal's low, rolling hills and flatlands.

Covering an area of 75,955 square miles (196,723 square kilometers), Senegal is about half the size of the U.S. state of California and 1.5 times the size of the country of England. Senegal has a long coastline to the west along the Atlantic Ocean. To the north, the Senegal River marks the border with Mauritania. To the east is Mali, and to the south are Guinea and Guinea-Bissau.

Senegal also surrounds The Gambia, one of Africa's smallest nations, on three sides. The fourth side of The Gambia consists of a small coastline.

Opposite: **In the Sahel region of Senegal, trees are mixed with grasslands.**

Senegal's Geographic Features

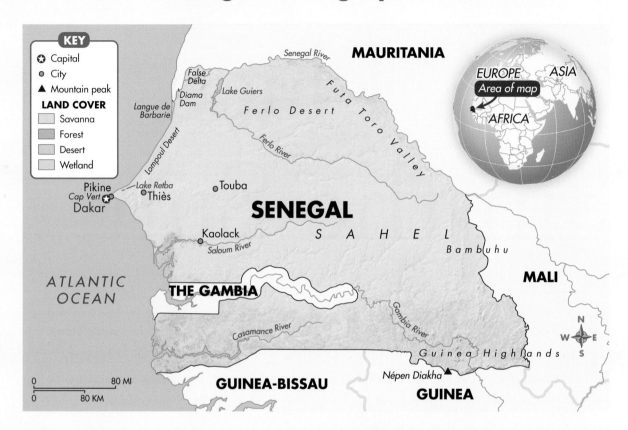

Area: 75,955 square miles (196,723 sq km)

Length of Coastline: 330 miles (531 km)

Highest Elevation: Near Népen Diakha, 1,906 feet (581 m) above sea level

Lowest Elevation: Sea level along the Atlantic Ocean

Longest River: Senegal River, about 2,500 miles (4,000 km)

Average High Temperature: In Dakar, 77°F (25°C) in February, 87°F (31°C) in August

Average Low Temperature: In Dakar, 64°F (18°C) in February, 78°F (26°C) in August

Average Ocean Temperature: 83°F (28°C) in August; 69°F (21°C) in February

Average Annual Precipitation: 13 inches (33 cm) in the north; 61 inches (155 cm) in the southwest

Diverse Biomes

From desert plains to ocean beaches, Senegal contains nearly all the biomes found in West Africa. Biomes are the major types of environments of the world, such as desert, rain forest, or coral reef. In north-central Senegal is the Ferlo Desert, which occupies nearly one-third of the country. Near Senegal's northeastern border, the Ferlo meets the Sahel, a semiarid region of West Africa made up of sandy plains, dunes, and rocks. In a few areas of the Sahel are small seasonal creeks and patches of underground water where wild grasses and shrubby trees grow.

Senegal's savanna biome lies to the south of the desert grasslands and extends west to east. The savanna is a rolling grassland that receives enough rain to support wild grasses and some trees, but not enough rain to create a forest. During the

About one-third of the land in Senegal is desert.

rainy season, the savanna's grasses are a major food source for a wide variety of animals. But during times of drought, wildfires fueled by dry grass threaten the land. In southeastern Senegal, rolling plains rise slightly to reach the country's highest elevation at just 1,906 feet (581 meters). The unnamed location is near the remote village of Népen Diakha. Along the southern borders lies a band of rich, tropical forest fed by rivers and heavy rainfall.

Sandy beaches, river mouths, and open surf mark the long coastline of Senegal. Like the rest of the country, the coastline is mostly flat, except for the Cap Vert peninsula on the

The rocky Cap Vert peninsula is the westernmost part of Africa.

Senegalese people water young trees that will be planted as part of the Great Green Wall.

The Great Green Wall

The Sahara Desert is a vast swath of rock and sand that cuts all the way across North Africa. As the climate changes and summers grow hotter, the desert is expanding. The shifting sand has farmers, herders, and government officials very concerned. Leaders of Senegal and twenty other countries near the Sahara have formed an alliance to combat the possible environmental disaster. They are building a "Great Green Wall" of drought-resistant trees.

When complete, this wall of trees will be 9 miles (14 km) wide and 4,750 miles (7,645 km) long. The trees will block the progress of the sand and provide food for livestock. More livestock means more fertilizer from manure to enrich the soil, which will help more crops grow. Every year since 2008, Senegalese workers have planted millions of seedlings along Senegal's 340-mile-long (545 km) section of the wall.

northern end. The peninsula is made of solid volcanic rock and features some towering rock formations. Cap Vert curves south toward the mainland and protects the capital and port city of Dakar by blocking waves and wind.

Rivers to the Sea

Four main rivers run east to west across Senegal before emptying into the Atlantic Ocean. The northernmost river is the Senegal. It rises in the Guinea Highlands and flows west between Mauritania and Senegal. Although the landscape is mostly dry, irrigation systems and dams help millions of citizens farm the land. As the river nears the town of Dagana, the ground is so flat that the river spreads into what is called the False Delta, creating numerous islands. The city of Saint-Louis rests on one of these islands. A sandspit called the Langue de

In Senegal, many rivers and streams snake toward the sea.

Lac Rose

There are few lakes in Senegal, but one of the most notable is Lake Retba, which local people call Lac Rose. Located just north of the Cap Vert peninsula, the lake is extremely salty. Salt is mined at the lake, and workers must cover themselves in thick oil to protect their skin. A strain of salt-loving bacteria lives in the lake, and combined with the hot sun and the extreme mineral content, a rare chemical reaction occurs that turns the lake a brilliant pink.

During the dry season, roughly November to April, Lac Rose has a strong red color. In the rainy season, the lake's unusual color is less noticeable.

Barbarie separates the city from the Atlantic Ocean. Between Saint-Louis and the mouth of the Senegal River lies a large estuary, where salt water and fresh water mix, providing a home to a vast variety of plants and animals.

The Saloum River runs across the center of the country through mangrove forests. The delta at the mouth of the river is thick with palms, vines, and other tropical plants. Its waterways loop and curl and twist into a complex maze of marshlands, fresh water, and salt water. The Gambia River also rises in the Guinea Highlands and flows across southeast Senegal before flowing west through The Gambia to the Atlantic. The Gambia River flows through a lush valley and provides a habitat for fish and animals such as hippopotamuses. South of the Gambia River runs the Casamance River, which rises in southern Senegal and flows for 190 miles (300 km) through a flat plain of rich vegetation. At its mouth are a vast delta and wetlands.

Protecting the Environment

Senegal has many environmental challenges. Much of the native forests have been cut to use for fuel or logged illegally and shipped overseas. Natural grasslands have been overgrazed, lax farming practices have eroded the soil, and mining operations have polluted rivers and streams. Overfishing in both fresh water and salt water has not only depleted the fish humans consume but has also threatened animals that rely on fish for food. Yet Senegal is working to preserve the environment. The country has established several national parks and refuges.

The rich wetlands of Djoudj National Bird Sanctuary along the banks of the lower Senegal River are a haven for millions of birds, many of which migrate across the Sahara. At the southern end of the Langue de Barbarie sandspit is Langue de Barbarie National Park, an island refuge for migratory birds and endangered sea turtles. West of Dakar lie several volcanic rock islands which make up the Îles des Madeleines National Park. The islands, Sarpan being the largest, have steep cliffs created by millions of years of pounding wind and surf. Saloum Delta National Park is a vast wilderness of beaches, tide flats, wetlands, islands, and mangrove swamps. The park is a major sanctuary for migrating birds and rare marine animals.

Senegal's largest and wildest national park is Niokolo-Koba National Park, situated by the Gambia River in the southeast. The park encompasses savanna, forests, and freshwater wetlands. Many large mammals live within the park, including baboons and hippopotamuses. The southernmost park is Basse Casamance National Park. It is located in an area of political

unrest and cut off from most of the rest of Senegal by The Gambia. Yet the native savanna and lush rain forests are protected and continue to provide homes for several dozens of animal species, including leopards, crocodiles, and monkeys.

Climate

Senegal basically has two seasons—wet and dry. The rainy season lasts from about June to September or October. The amount of rain varies depending upon the region. The Sahel region receives between 10 and 15 inches (25 and 40 centimeters) of rain each year, while the southern region receives between 40 and 60 inches (100 and 150 cm). Rainfall on the coast measures about 20 inches (50 cm) a year.

Niokola-Koba National Park provides habitat for about 330 species of birds. These include red-throated bee-eaters, which nest in holes in riverbanks.

Senegalese cool down in the ocean on a hot day on Gorée Island.

Temperatures also vary depending on the region. The arid Sahel region is often hot during the day, reaching temperatures as high as 104 degrees Fahrenheit (40 degrees Celsius), but can drop to around 55°F (13°C) at night. The southern region is both hot and humid. Temperatures stay steady at about 85°F (30°C) all year. The coastal region enjoys ocean breezes that cool the air. Temperatures range from 65°F to 80°F (18°C to 27°C) in winter up to about 85°F (30°C) in summer.

When the heat rises, the rains fall. But when the temperature cools slightly and the dry season begins, heavy winds, called Harmattan winds, blast in from the Sahara. The winds carry thick, swirling clouds of dust. People cough and wheeze and cover their faces with scarves and masks. Animals choke on the dust and crops can fail because the dust blocks out the sun.

Urban Landscapes

Dakar, the capital, is the largest city in Senegal, with about 2.5 million residents. Some of its suburbs also have large populations. Pikine, the nation's second-largest city, has a population of almost 875,000.

Touba, home to more than 500,000 people, is the third-largest city in Senegal. It is a bustling commercial hub in the nation's interior. It is also an important cultural and religious center. The city's largest mosque is a major pilgrimage site.

Thiès, with a population of about 320,000, is located near the Cap Vert peninsula. It is the ancestral home of the Serer-Noon ethnic group. The city supports many industries such as traditional tapestry weaving. It is also a market hub for the region's farmers. Thiès is the site of several universities and a large military base.

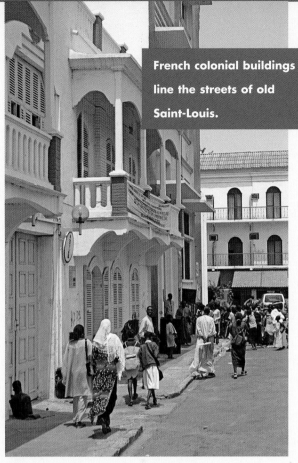

French colonial buildings line the streets of old Saint-Louis.

The Great Mosque of Touba can accommodate seven thousand worshippers.

The fifth-largest city, Kaolack, has a population of more than 230,000. Located on the Saloum River, Kaolack is an important market and transportation hub for southeastern Senegal. Many agricultural products leave Kaolack via waterways, roads, and trains.

Saint-Louis, now home to about 210,000 people, was once the colonial capital of all of French West Africa. In many neighborhoods, historic European homes and buildings remain. The city is located on a lush island in the Senegal River. The city boasts theaters, restaurants, museums, and many arts and music festivals.

CHAPTER 3

Wildlife and Habitats

I N SENEGAL'S DRY DESERT GRASSLANDS, SAVANNAS, tropical forests, rivers, and coastline lives a vibrant variety of plants and animals. The nation is home to more than 3,500 species of plants and trees, and huge numbers of species of animals, including 664 types of birds, about 180 species of mammals, more than fifty species each of amphibians and reptiles, and hundreds of kinds of insects.

Opposite: **A green monkey feeds on the flowers of a kapok tree in Niokolo-Koba National Park. The monkey gets its name from the greenish tinge of its fur.**

Plant Life

The northern part of Senegal is a dry sandy plain, broken up occasionally by isolated trees, thorny bushes, and hardy grasses. For a few months during the rainy season, the grasses grow lush and the trees and bushes leaf out. The landscape becomes ideal for grazing domesticated animals. Wild animals, too, come to the region to forage for food. People and animals make careful use of their short-lived bounty. Using traditional methods, people harvest leaves, bark, fruit, and wood for use in daily living.

The baobab tree, found in many regions, survives where few others can. Some specimens are more than a thousand years old. The baobab grows anywhere from 15 to 80 feet (4.5 to 24 m) tall. It has an enormous trunk where it stores water during the rainy season, and branches that spread wide, resembling a mass of thin tentacles. Come the dry season, when most other plants are bare, the baobab produces a nutritious fruit. Other fruit trees found in the Sahel and savanna

A man harvests bark and sap from an incense tree.

Tree of Many Blessings

The national tree of Senegal is the baobab. The tree provides food, shelter, and medicine. People use the wood for fuel and the bark for making baskets and rope. They grind the roots to make dyes and medicines. Baobabs provide rare shade for people and animals, and many villages are built around them. Legends say the trees are magical and protect spirits that live within them. The revered baobab tree goes by many names, such as the monkey-bread tree, the upside-down tree, and the tree of life.

The baobab tree stores water in its trunk, which sometimes grows to 30 feet (9 m) across.

are the bush mango and the tamarind. Both are used in cooking and in making medicines.

More than eighty tree and shrub species live in Senegal's savanna region. A common type is the acacia tree. Acacias are able to survive very dry conditions and extreme temperatures. The acacia grows quickly, reaching heights of 40 feet (12 m) in less than ten years. Acacia trees are important resources for people of the savanna. The umbrella thorn acacia produces a yellow flower and a long seedpod. The seeds are eaten, the bark is used to make dye, and the wood is harvested to make furniture and houses. Another species, the gum arabic acacia, produces a sticky sap called gum arabic. For centuries, gum arabic has been used as an ingredient in glue, paint, and medicine.

The gnarly shea tree is found across the savanna. Although it takes about fifteen years to produce a flower and fruit, once it does it will produce for at least one hundred years more. The fruit is very nutritious and an important part of the Senegalese diet. Shea is pounded into butter and made into cooking oil. It is also turned into body lotions prized around the world. Other plants found in the savanna include the African locust bean tree, the desert date, okra, hibiscus, and elephant grass. Elephant grass is so named because it grows up to 10 feet (3 m) tall.

About 45 percent of Senegal is forested. Most of the forests are located in the southern part of the country. About 18 percent of Senegal's forests are old growth trees. The kapok, or ceiba, tree is a powerful presence in southern forests. The tree towers over all others growing as much as 13 feet (4 m) taller a year and topping out at about 200 feet (60 m). Kapok trees are known for their massive root system and fluffy flowers. Although the pink-and-white flowers are beautiful, they smell foul. Bats are attracted to the odor and pollinate the trees. Humans also have many uses for the tree. People gather the silky, cotton-like fibers attached to the seeds and use them to stuff mattresses. The oily seeds are used in making soap, and the bark is used to make medicines. Carvers produce canoes and sculptures from the wood. Many people call kapok the silk-cotton tree, but the Senegalese call it *fromager* (French for "cheese-like") because the wood is soft and easy to carve.

As many as forty-five species of wild fruit tree grow in southeastern Senegal, near Niokolo-Koba National Park. These include Senegalese custard-apple, southern ficus, bush mango, African fan palm, tamarind, and African peach. The kigelia tree, commonly called the sausage tree, bears a foul-smelling flower and a sausage-shaped fruit, which people use for medicine and skin lotions. Other trees and plants found in the southeast include Senegalese mahogany, rosewood, tallow tree, and African birch.

Forests in southwestern Senegal are the thickest, wettest, and most humid in the country. On the forest floor grow vines, lianas, orchids, bromeliads, mosses, and lichens. Lianas are vine-like plants that sink their roots into tree trunks and climb upward in search of sunlight. Eventually they kill their host tree. Orchids and bromeliads are plants with brilliantly colored flowers that grow in low light. Along the Casamance

The kapok has huge buttress roots, which help stabilize the massive tree.

and Souman Rivers grow thick stands of palms, kapoks, bamboo, African teak, and wild cashew.

Trees common along the coast are palms and mangroves. Prized oil palms grow in the south. Their seeds are used in making palm oil and palm wine. Vast stands of mangroves grow along much of the coast. They grow in brackish water—a mixture of fresh water and salt water. Their roots extend from the upper branches down to form a thick knot, both above and below the water's surface. Mangroves protect land and beaches from eroding. The roots capture mud and debris from the movement of the tides, forming swampland. Mangrove swamps protect young fish and other small animals from predators.

Life in Water

Senegal's various habitats serve as home to a great diversity of wildlife, including an abundance of both freshwater and saltwater fish. In the ocean, fishers harvest sardine, grouper, snapper, sea bass, mackerel, and West African goatfish. Large game fish include barracuda, jackfish, and tuna. Living on the seabed are oysters, lobsters, and octopus. Fishers also harvest shellfish such as clams and shrimp. Several shark species live in the water, including nurse shark and tiger shark. Freshwater fish found in Senegal's nutrient-rich rivers include lampeye, goby, tetra, tiger fish, moonfish, pike, tilapia, and the Senegal giraffe catfish, which is found only in Senegal.

Senegal's marine mammals include harbor porpoises, spinner dolphins, and orcas, which are also called killer whales. In the Casamance River live rare river dolphins that can be

A man harvests oysters that are attached to mangrove roots.

seen diving across the bows of fishers' canoes. A number of whales migrate offshore, including minke, sei, sperm, and the endangered humpback.

The West African manatee is an endangered mammal found among mangroves and in shallow water. Shaped like a torpedo, the West African manatee measures 10 to 14 feet (3 to 4 m) long and weighs up to 1,100 pounds (500 kilograms). Manatees are herbivores (plant eating) and consume about 50 pounds (23 kg) of mangrove leaves a day. Another large marine mammal, the dugong, eats underwater grasses and can stay submerged for up to six minutes. The slow-moving dugongs have been easy targets for hunters after their meat, skin, bones, teeth, and oil. Today, dugongs and manatees are protected by the government.

Reptiles and Amphibians

More than one hundred species of reptiles and amphibians can be found in Senegal. There are more than fifty species of snakes, including the African rock python, which can grow to 20 feet (6 m) long and strangle and devour an antelope. Lizards, skinks, geckos, and chameleons are common in many parts of the country. The largest lizards are monitors. The Nile monitor is a strong swimmer, able rock climber, and fast runner. Monitors capture and poison their prey, which

The green mamba is one of nine species of venomous snakes that live in Senegal. It spends most of its time in trees.

Against All Odds

Five species of endangered sea turtles lay their eggs along Senegal's coast: leatherback, green, hawksbill, loggerhead, and olive ridley. Leatherbacks are the largest, with some weighing more than 1,000 pounds (450 kg). Female sea turtles drag their bodies awkwardly onto beaches at night, dig nests, lay their eggs, and return to the ocean. Although adult sea turtles are immense, young sea turtles are very vulnerable. When the turtles hatch, they crawl from their nests and make a solitary journey to the sea. Predators are never far away. Few turtles survive to adulthood. Their existence is threatened from multiple causes. Humans eat the eggs and meat and use the turtles' hard shells to make tools, crafts, and jewelry. Animals dig up the turtle eggs and hatchlings. Predator fish and birds attack. Environmental problems such as water pollution, beach erosion, and human development also endanger the sea turtles.

The hawksbill sea turtle gets its name from the shape of its mouth.

includes fish, frogs, snakes, birds, and small mammals. Of the four species of crocodile that live in Africa, three are found in Senegal. They are the West African crocodile, the slender-snouted crocodile, and the West African dwarf crocodile.

Many different toads, frogs, and salamanders live in Senegal. African bullfrogs live near water and burrow in mud. They can withstand extreme heat and freezing cold, but when temperatures become too harsh, they hibernate.

Turtles and tortoises are found throughout the country. The largest tortoise in Africa is the African spurred tortoise. It has a thick skin to hold water in dry conditions. Endangered sea turtles come ashore on Senegal's beaches each year to lay their eggs.

Insects, Butterflies, and Moths

Come the end of the rainy season, insects, butterflies, and moths appear everywhere in Senegal. There are dragonflies, crickets, grasshoppers, praying mantises, beetles, and ants. One species, called the African ant, travels in massive groups and can overwhelm and devour large creatures. Other dangerous insects include the tsetse fly, whose bite can cause sleeping sickness, and mosquitoes that can carry serious diseases such as malaria, yellow fever, and dengue fever.

Birds

From desert birds like sandgrouse, and savanna birds such as falcons and weaverbirds, to seabirds like storm petrels and oystercatchers, Senegal has an amazing bird population. More than 550 species make their home there for either part or all of the year. More than three million migrating birds, including spoonbills, avocets, and warblers, stop over and breed in the wetlands of the Djoudj National Bird Sanctuary in the Senegal River delta. Most of the migrant birds begin their journey in the Arctic and fly over the Sahara Desert. The first sources of fresh water the birds encounter are the wetlands of Djoudj, which is considered one of the top bird refuges in the world.

The Ferlo Desert national wildlife preserve is host to hornbills, bustards, raptors, and one of Africa's last remaining populations of wild ostriches. Other national parks provide safe nesting places for birds such as the rose-ringed parakeet, spotted cuckoo, and the brilliant green turaco, known as the plantain-eater. At home on the savanna are colorful Senegal parrots, golden sparrows,

and vultures. Coastal areas and river mouths are rich breeding grounds for wading birds such as herons, egrets, cranes, and flamingos, as well as plovers, gulls, and terns.

Pelicans fly at Djoudj National Bird Sanctuary. The main food of pelicans is fish, which they scoop up with their giant beaks.

Mammals

Senegal is rich in mammal life. More than seventy species live in Niokolo-Koba National Park alone, and elsewhere there are many more. Animals roaming Niokolo-Koba include leopards, lions, African wild dogs, aardvarks, antelopes, and in dwindling numbers, elephants.

In the savanna live animals such as gazelles, giraffes, jackals, hyenas, and warthogs. Like its name implies, the warthog is related to a pig. These large creatures have four tusks. Although they look ferocious, they are herbivores that use their tusks for digging up roots, making dens, and guarding their offspring. When it is hot, warthogs wallow in mud to cool off. Hippopotamuses also wallow in rivers and muddy ponds throughout the day. They, too, are herbivores. They are extremely dangerous, however, and will kill whatever creature ventures near, including crocodiles, monitor lizards, and humans.

Warthogs have large bumps on their heads, which serve as protective pads during combat.

The Senegal Lion

Senegal's coat of arms bears the image of the national symbol, the baobab tree, and a lion. The West African lion, also called the Senegal lion, is critically endangered. In many areas where it once thrived, it has now disappeared. There are thought to be roughly four hundred Senegal lions left in Africa. Those remaining in Senegal live within the protected areas of Niokolo-Koba National Park.

Among Senegalese, the lion is a symbol of strength.

The forests of southern Senegal were once home to many types of primates, the order of animals that includes humans, apes, and monkeys. Various types of monkeys, including patas, western red colobus, vervet, and mangabey, still live in these forests. But many of the larger primates, including baboons, gorillas, and chimpanzees, are mostly found only inside Niokolo-Koba National Park. Gorillas have become particularly rare. The hoots and calls of chimpanzees can be heard throughout the park and the surrounding forest, but they are also endangered.

CHAPTER 4

A Proud Heritage

HUNDREDS OF THOUSANDS OF YEARS AGO, EARLY humans migrated into Senegal from other parts of Africa. They lived in small groups and hunted animals and gathered wild fruits, nuts, seeds, and grasses. Ancient remnants of tools made from stone, bone, and horn have been found throughout the Sahel and along the rivers to the coast. Later societies made tools from stone and iron, pottery from mud and clay, and beads from shells and wood. Over time, people developed farming, fishing, mining, and boatbuilding skills. They began to decorate their pottery and tools, make wood carvings, and paint images on walls and rock.

Opposite: **The Wolof people have been making elegant gold jewelry for centuries. Wolof women typically wore gold, such as this pendant, while men were more likely to wear silver.**

Early Kingdoms

Knowledge of the history of Senegal's people has been passed down through generations of formal storytellers, called griots.

Stone Circles

Between the third century BCE and the sixteenth century CE, ancient Senegalese stonecutters built some of the world's most impressive prehistoric monuments, known as the Senegambian stone circles. The monuments are made of tens of thousands of pieces of solid stone positioned into more than a thousand circles. Each stone is about 6.5 feet (2 m) high.

Mystery surrounds the stone circles. Since the circles were constructed over the course of about two thousand years, experts believe that constructing them was an important rite or tradition. The stones were cut from quarries and carried overland to sites along the Gambia River. The circles appear to surround burial mounds. Many mounds seem to be mass burials, such as would be needed after a battle or disease epidemic.

The first written records came from traveling traders from North Africa, people known as the Berbers. The name Senegal is believed to be derived from the name of a Berber group, the Zenaga. Berbers crossed the Sahara in caravans of camels to trade salt, dates, brass, and iron for West African gold and elephant ivory. Traders also exchanged humans whom they had enslaved. It was common for enemies to capture those they defeated and enslave them. Additionally, people in powerful positions frequently enslaved people who owed them money. Some of the people enslaved were able to work off their debts or buy their freedom.

Arab traders from southwest Asia followed the Berber trade routes and traded with groups in the Sahel and along the Senegal River. As trading communities grew, kingdoms formed. Beginning in the seventh century, in what is now Mauritania and eastern Senegal, the Ghana Empire rose to power. Considered the "Land of Gold" by North African

Berber traders would sometimes use hundreds of camels on their journeys across the deserts of North Africa.

The Tukulor people were known for their distinctive hairstyles and headdresses.

and Arab traders, Ghana was the first of several empires to emerge in West Africa. It was ruled by the Soninke people, who established a well-organized government and amassed a large army. The ruler, or *ghana*, gained enormous wealth by requiring traders and gold miners to pay taxes to him in gold.

The earliest kingdom within Senegal was the Tekrur kingdom, formed by the Fulbe and Tukulor people. The Fulbe were nomads, people who moved from place to place and herded goats and cattle. They settled throughout West Africa. Many intermarried with the Tukulor people who had villages in the Futa Toro valley of the Senegal River. In the tenth century, traders from a Berber group called the Almoravids made contact with the Tekrur kingdom. They wanted to trade for goods such as grain and gold, but they also wanted to force the kingdom's rulers to convert to their religion, Islam. By the eleventh century, the Almoravids were successful. As the first Senegalese to adopt Islam, the people of the Tekrur kingdom spread its teachings to other groups. The kingdom flourished between the ninth and twelfth centuries.

The Almoravids established settlements within the Ghana Empire, though they were unable to convert the Ghana ruler to Islam. As newcomers from other groups came under Ghanaian control, skirmishes became more frequent. Meanwhile, the Almoravids continued to mount wars in the name of Islam. Eventually, the Almoravids triumphed, and by the eleventh century, the Ghana Empire had gone into a steep decline.

The fall of the Ghana Empire left an opening for another kingdom to take hold. The Mali Empire was founded by the Malinke people, who were middlemen in the trans-Sahara gold trade. In the twelfth century, Muslim clerics and scholars began accompanying the traders. The clerics converted people to Islam. The scholars introduced their written Arabic language and numbering system. Cities within the Mali Empire became centers of learning and religious thought. At its peak, the Mali Empire was one of the largest in the world. It included most of what is now Senegal, Mauritania, Guinea,

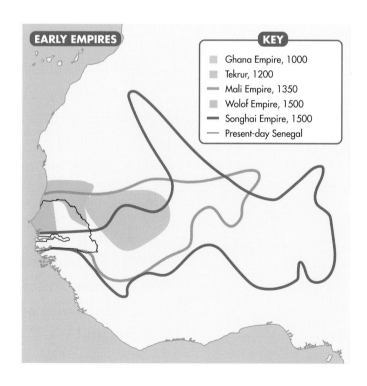

EARLY EMPIRES

KEY

Ghana Empire, 1000
Tekrur, 1200
Mali Empire, 1350
Wolof Empire, 1500
Songhai Empire, 1500
Present-day Senegal

Mali, Burkina Faso, Niger, Nigeria, and The Gambia. With its enormous caches of gold, the Mali Empire was also one of the world's wealthiest empires.

Conflict and Upheaval

The Mali Empire had overpowered many chiefdoms and smaller kingdoms. The Malinke, Fulbe, Soninke, Tukulor, and Wolof groups all paid taxes to the *mansa*, or emperor. Eventually, these groups broke from the Mali Empire. In 1360, the Wolofs were the first to gain independence from Mali. Their kingdom had been founded in the thirteenth century by Ndiadiane Ndiaye, the son of a Tukulor holy man. He became legendary for his bravery and mystical powers. By the fourteenth century, the Wolof Empire spread from the Senegal to the Gambia Rivers. Its wealth stemmed from the vast Bambuhu gold fields in eastern Senegal.

In the late fourteenth century, infighting among the Malian royals weakened the empire and other kingdoms took advantage. Eventually, the Songhai toppled the capital of Mali. The Songhai Empire became the last and the largest of the West African empires. It included what are now Burkina Faso, The Gambia, Guinea, Mali, Mauritania, Niger, and Senegal.

The African Nightmare

Word of West Africa's immense wealth made its way to Europe. In the fifteenth century, Europeans began targeting the region. In 1445, Portuguese merchants landed on the Cap Vert Peninsula. They established small settlements along the

Wolof people travel across Dakar Bay in pirogues.

coast and on Gorée Island, and soon began sailing up the Senegal River.

Portugal and Spain operated sugar plantations along the African coast in Madeira and the Canary Islands. Planters could not find enough laborers and began enslaving Africans from the mainland to work. To meet their demands, Portuguese slaving merchants raided African villages and captured people to sell to plantation owners. The Portuguese later realized that they could transport more people to slave markets by encouraging Africans on the coast to raid villages in the interior. The Portuguese traded guns, wine, and other European goods for captured prisoners.

By the early sixteenth century, the Portuguese had formed colonies in Brazil, where they established sugar plantations. Human slave trafficking increased dramatically. In 1536, the Portuguese began shipping enslaved Africans across the

Atlantic from Gorée Island. Later in the sixteenth century, France, Spain, and Britain had established colonies in North America. These colonies also required intensive labor to produce their cash crops of sugar and cotton. The slave trade expanded. Gorée Island became a major slave port. The Portuguese and Dutch traded control of the island until it was seized by England in 1664.

By the seventeenth century, England and France were in a battle for global dominance. The two nations set their sights on colonizing and acquiring foreign possessions. Africa, with its vast natural resources, attracted both nations. The French arrived in Senegal in 1638. They established a post

European powers often battled for control of Gorée Island. Here, English ships attack the island when it was under French control.

A visitor is silhouetted in the Door of No Return on Gorée Island.

Door of No Return

In 1776, on the rocky island of Gorée, the Dutch constructed a fort, called the House of Slaves, to keep Africans whom they had enslaved. The Africans were brought to the island to await ships that would take them across the Atlantic to a life of slavery in Brazil, the Caribbean Islands, or the United States. Each person was chained to a heavy metal ball. Waters around the island were so deep that any attempt to escape would result in drowning.

European merchants and administrators lived on the top floor of the building. On the bottom floors, the captives were kept in hot, dark, and filthy conditions. Men were chained together. They were assigned a value based on their age and strength. Women were kept in separate rooms and valued for their youth and the shape of their bodies. Children were kept away from their parents and were assigned a value based on their health and the quality of their teeth. Captives, bound for a cruel fate, left the House of Slaves by passing through what is known as the Door of No Return.

Today, the House of Slaves is an important historic site. It is a memorial to those who suffered enslavement and a reminder of an ugly past built upon greed and hatred. When U.S. president Barack Obama visited Gorée, he said, "This is a testament to when we're not vigilant in defense of human rights what can happen."

A Proud Heritage

KEY
○ French settlement
○ British settlement
○ Portuguese settlement
— Present-day Senegal

Saint-Louis

Gorée

Bathurst

Cacheu
Bissau

EUROPEAN SETTLEMENTS, 19th CENTURY

at the mouth of the Senegal River. They moved their base of operations to the more secure island they called Saint-Louis in 1659. In 1677, they seized Gorée Island from the English.

The French, at first, were after West Africa's riches, such as gold, ivory, textiles, ostrich feathers, and kola nuts. But France had possessions in the Caribbean where they had established sugar plantations. They, too, began enslaving West Africans, and during the eighteenth century, the French became the third-largest slave traders. In 1818, the French government outlawed the slave trade. However, French slaving ships continued to operate illegally for more than twenty years. By the end of the slave trade, nearly two million Senegalese captives had boarded French ships through the ports of Gorée Island and Saint-Louis.

French Colonization

In 1854, France appointed a civil engineer and army major, Louis Faidherbe, governor of Senegal. Faidherbe began building forts and railways. He directed military expeditions into the interior with the goal of taking land from the local people. Faidherbe was willing to use force. Many Senegalese communities and kingdoms resisted.

To meet his aims, Faidherbe ordered more troops and weapons from France. He formed an infantry of Senegalese soldiers who were either very poor or enslaved. These soldiers were sent ahead to villages to coerce the leaders into giving away their territory.

One of the local leaders they confronted was a Tukulor Islamic scholar named Umar Tal. He had visited the Muslim holy land in a religious pilgrimage. When he returned, he established an imamate, a government led by an imam, or Muslim holy man. Umar Tal built an Islamic state in West Africa, an empire that covered parts of what are now Senegal, Mali, and Guinea.

Faidherbe built a fort in Médine, along the Senegal River in the Futa Toro valley. But Umar Tal was intent on protecting his territory. His army overran the French fort, but the French reclaimed it a few months later. Both Umar Tal and Faidherbe were determined. In 1859, the French army,

Louis Faidherbe began his career as an engineer but quickly became the colonial governor of Senegal. As governor, he greatly expanded France's West African empire.

Queen of the Women's Army

In 1846, Ndate Yalla Mbodj was crowned queen of the Waalo kingdom, a state within the Wolof Empire. Men often left villages to work or go into battle; the women who remained at home were responsible for protecting children, elders, and village property. The women were required to have military training. Ndate Yalla Mbodj led her women's army into battle against Faidherbe's French soldiers. She insisted that Faidherbe respect her power and refused him passage onto her lands.

She wrote to him that the land was hers: "There is nobody who can claim that that country belongs to them; it belongs to me only. I did not sell this country to anybody. I did not entrust it to anybody, nor to any white person." Faidherbe responded by sending troops to burn and loot villages and steal livestock. Ndate Yalla Mbodj lost that battle, but she and her soldiers continued resisting the French into the twentieth century. A statue to her bravery stands in Dagana, a city near Saint-Louis.

Ndate Yalla Mbodj was a leader in the resistance to French colonialism. She is always depicted smoking a pipe.

made up mostly of Senegalese fighters, defeated the Tukulor army. Faidherbe's aggressive tactics changed Senegal from a region of isolated trading posts, villages, and small chiefdoms into a major political and military force within West Africa.

Colonization did little to improve the lives of the Senegalese. French colonies were required to support themselves. Plantations were established. The local people were forced to plant and harvest crops that could be sold at a premium in Europe, including peanuts, gum arabic, cotton, kola nuts, palm oil, and shea butter. People were forced to raise ostriches for feathers, mine salt and gold, and kill wild animals for their hides and ivory. Workers were paid little, if at all. Many were ordered to leave their villages and move to areas where the cash crops grew best. Most people no longer had control over their land or the time to raise enough crops to feed themselves.

New Boundaries

During the nineteenth century, more than a dozen European nations laid claims in Africa. The period was called the Scramble for Africa. In 1884 and 1885, the nations met in Berlin, Germany, to discuss how to divide up the continent. Lines were drawn creating political boundaries, which took no account of traditional ethnic territories. No Africans were invited to the conference. They had no say in how their lands were mapped. During the conference, France was given control of the areas that are now Benin, Algeria, Guinea, Niger, and Senegal.

By 1890, the French established borders between these areas.

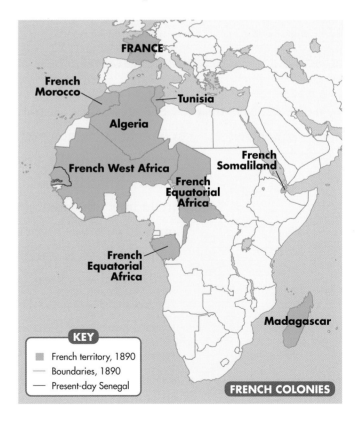

By the 1800s, Saint-Louis was a thriving city.

Senegal was split into two political parts—the colony and four communes, which were regions of special status. The communes were in the major commercial centers of Saint-Louis, Gorée, Rufisque, and Dakar. People living in the communes, including educated Africans and mixed-race people, were granted rights as French citizens. They were allowed to elect a representative to the French parliament.

Senegal was French West Africa's most successful colony. Its cash crops filled the government's coffers, and the port cities of Dakar and Saint-Louis bustled with activity. Saint-Louis was the seat of government for all French West Africa. But by 1902, Dakar had developed into such a prosperous port that the capital shifted there.

The International Stage

In 1914 in Europe, a single incident—an assassination and its aftermath—set World War I in motion. During the war, France, Britain, Belgium, and Russia opposed Germany, Austria, Hungary, Bulgaria, and Turkey. France turned to its African colonies to recruit soldiers. All Senegalese men except for the privileged citizens of the communes were required to enlist in the military. Battalions of Senegalese were sent to fight on European battlefields. More than 170,000 Senegalese fought in the four-year war.

Senegalese soldiers in France during World War I. More than thirty thousand Senegalese were killed in the war.

In 1939, Europeans again went to war. Nazi Germany invaded Poland, and Britain and France declared war on Germany. World War II had begun. In 1940, Germany invaded and occupied France. They allowed some French officials to govern the nation from a city called Vichy. The Vichy regime, aligned with Germany, took control of French West Africa and established Dakar as its stronghold.

French people fighting the Vichy regime and Germany were called the Free French. In September 1940, British and Free French navies attacked Dakar. They were not successful, and the battle of Dakar ended two days later. In 1942, however, the armies of Free France and Britain invaded North Africa and convinced Dakar to change allegiance. Tens of thousands of Senegalese soldiers were recruited to liberate France from Nazi Germany.

Independence and After

Senegal's own fight for independence began just after World War II ended in 1945. The people of Senegal deeply resented how they were treated by their colonial rulers. A number of Senegalese soldiers mutinied and were shot by French troops. The violence enraged the Senegalese. In 1947 and 1948, they held a massive railway strike that shut the economy down. They demanded wages equal to those paid to whites.

In 1956, the French government passed a law giving its territories the right to govern themselves. And in 1960, Senegal became a completely independent nation.

As an independent nation, Léopold Senghor was elected

The First President

Léopold Senghor, Senegal's first president, was the son of a wealthy father of the Serer ethnic group. His mother, a member of the Fulbe ethnic group, was Catholic and sent him to private school. There, he learned French and excelled at his studies. He earned a scholarship to study literature in France and became an accomplished author and poet.

During World War II he was captured and imprisoned in a concentration camp. He wrote some of his most important poems during this time. Upon his release, Senghor was appointed to the National Assembly. Later, he was elected mayor of the Senegalese city of Thiès. When Senegal became independent, Senghor was unanimously elected president. The economy

Léopold Senghor first began representing Senegal in the National Assembly in France in 1946.

prospered under his guidance and the arts thrived. When he resigned after twenty years, he said it was because he needed to write poetry.

president. He served for five terms. Senghor's presidency was one of the most peaceful of any of the former colonies in Africa, except for one crisis with his prime minister, Mamadou Dia. In December 1962, Dia attempted a takeover of the government in a coup, but he was halted, tried, and sentenced to prison. The office of prime minister was removed from the constitution. Senghor reinstated it in 1970, and then in a show of unity, appointed Abdou Diouf, a member of another political party, prime minister. Thereafter, Senghor's presidency was focused on developing agriculture, modernizing infrastructure, and forming closer ties with neighboring countries. He and his successors believed in what was called African socialism, a form of government that promoted equality among ethnic groups, communal ownership of land, and freedom of religion.

More Recent Times

Senghor resigned in 1980 to hand the presidency to Abdou Diouf, who served for another twenty years. Diouf's presidency began with the continuation of peace and growth, but within a year, crises developed. The first was a decision to send Senegalese troops across the border with The Gambia to help prevent a coup against The Gambia's president. This led to a union between the two nations, called the Senegambia Confederation. The two nations agreed to share military troops, a single currency, and foreign relations. The confederation fell apart a decade later.

In 1989, a border dispute between Senegalese farmers and Mauritanian herders exploded into violence that left thousands of people dead or wounded. Nearly a quarter million people on either side of the border were displaced or deported. The conflict subsided after two years, with the countries agreeing to share the borderland, and in the following years many of the deportees were allowed to return.

One of the longest-running conflicts in Africa is in the Casamance region in the southern part of Senegal. The conflict is led by a rebel group, Movement of Democratic Forces of Casamance (MFDC). Since 1982, many people in Casamance have wanted to separate from the rest of Senegal. They believe the national government does not give them adequate economic support. They also resent that most government workers are from the Muslim Wolof ethnic group, whereas most people in Casamance belong to the Catholic Diola group. Casamance is physically separated from the rest of Senegal by Gambia. It takes more than twenty-four hours to drive to Dakar from Ziguinchor, the capital of Casamance. For more than thirty-five years, the MFDC and Senegalese troops have fought. Land mines have been set in farmland, people have been kidnapped, and more than five thousand people have been killed. Despite ongoing violence, many believe the conflict is nearing an end. Far fewer rebels are active, and the separatist movement has become unpopular with the people. The national government is focusing on improving the region's economy. The land mines are being extracted, opening up farmland. Government and business leaders are working to improve the tourism industry, since Casamance has lush rain forest, clean rivers, and an unspoiled coastline. People hope that prosperity and a permanent peace are within reach.

Mauritanians await deportation from Senegal after a conflict along the border in 1989. More than a hundred thousand Mauritanians were sent back to their home country.

CHAPTER 5

An African Democracy

SENEGAL HAS A GOVERNMENT THAT IS WIDELY respected throughout Africa. The first president, Léopold Senghor, established a strong central government, which he believed would unite people regardless of their differences.

For the most part, this has proved true. Senegal has remained one of the most successful democratic governments within Africa, and the only one in the region that has never had a military coup.

Senegal's current constitution was adopted in 2001 and revised in 2016. The constitution grants citizens freedom of assembly, expression, opinion, and religion. It states that men and women are equal, and it bars discrimination. People have the right to public education, health, a clean environment, and private ownership of business and property.

Opposite: **A group called the Red Guard of Senegal is responsible for guarding the president.**

A Look at the Capital

Dakar is the largest city in Senegal and its capital. About 2.5 million people call the city home. Dakar rests on the Cap Vert peninsula. Hills and cliffs frame Dakar, and the city's beaches attract tourists and locals alike. The city enjoys milder weather than the rest of the country. Palm trees and flowers grow throughout the city.

Dakar is a sophisticated city. Downtown bustles with lively restaurants, museums, galleries, and theaters. There is colonial, contemporary, and Islamic architecture. The fashion and music scenes are internationally renowned. The city is a major shipping port and the center of finance and industry in the

Located at the end of the Cap Vert peninsula, Dakar is nearly surrounded by water.

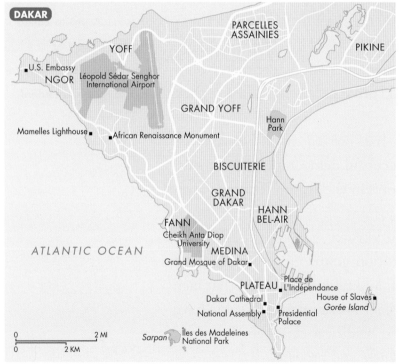

country. Dakar is also home to the country's largest university. Often called the University of Dakar, its formal name is Cheikh Anta Diop University, after a famed Senegalese physicist and anthropologist.

Atop a hill just outside the city stands a 160-foot-tall (49 m) bronze sculpture of an African man, woman, and child looking forward to a promising new future. Called the African Renaissance Monument, it has become a major attraction.

Former prime minister Macky Sall became president in 2012.

The Executive Branch

Senegal has three branches of government. The executive branch is led by the president, the prime minister, and a cabinet of ministers. The president, who is the head of state, is elected by the popular vote of the people. The prime minister is the head of government and is appointed by the president. The cabinet ministers are appointed by the prime minister on the recommendations of the president. Senegal's cabinet ministers oversee departments such as education, agriculture, energy, tourism, environment, and armed forces.

The Legislative Branch

The National Assembly is the legislative branch of the government. Starting when Senegal became independent in 1960, it included two houses—the National Assembly and the Senate. Then, in 2012, lawmakers voted to do away with the

The National Flag

The Senegalese flag was adopted in 1960.

Senegal's flag consists of three vertical bands of green, yellow, and red. Green signifies Islam, progress, and hope, yellow symbolizes natural wealth and economic progress, and red stands for sacrifice and determination. In the center of the yellow band is a small green five-pointed star, expressing unity and hope.

Senegal's National Government

Executive Branch
President
Prime Minister
Cabinet of Ministers

Legislative Branch
National Assembly
(165 members)

Judicial Branch
Court of Cassation
Court of Appeals
Administrative District Courts

Senate in an effort to save money. So presently, the legislative branch has only one house.

The National Assembly has 165 members. Of these, 105 are elected by popular vote. The other 60 are chosen by local governments or political party officials. Fifteen of the elected members represent people who live outside of Senegal, primarily in France, Spain, and Italy. Each member is elected to a five-year term. The National Assembly rarely sponsors legislation. Instead, it votes to approve bills introduced by the executive branch.

The Judicial Branch

The highest court in Senegal is the Court of Cassation. The court consists of a president and twelve judges who are

Members at a session of the National Assembly. Women hold more than 40 percent of the assembly seats.

appointed by the president on the recommendation of a judicial advisory council. Other federal courts include the Court of Appeals, the Council of State, and the Constitutional Court.

Lower courts include fourteen administrative district courts, which preside over Senegal's fourteen administrative districts. Below these courts are district courts, labor courts, and community councils.

An electoral worker opens a box where Senegalese placed their ballots to be counted.

Judges listen to testimony during the trial of Chadian leader Hissène Habré.

People enter the court building where the Extraordinary African Chamber meets.

International Law

In 2013, the government of Senegal and the African Union agreed to form a court named the Extraordinary African Chamber. The court, located in Dakar, was formed to try crimes committed outside of Senegal's borders. It was established to prosecute cases of genocide, crimes against humanity, war crimes, and torture. In 2016, the court convicted the former dictator of Chad, Hissène Habré, for crimes against humanity. He was sentenced to life in prison.

Regional and Local Government

Each of the fourteen administrative districts has a governor appointed by the president. The administrative districts are divided into departments, urban districts, and regional districts. In rural areas, councils are formed by representatives chosen from a group of villages. Dakar is managed by a municipal council.

Village elders from the Wolof ethnic group gather for a meeting.

The kora has twenty-one strings.

The National Anthem

Senegal's national anthem is called "Pincez Tous vos Koras, Frappez les Balafons," which translates to "Pluck Your Koras, Strike the Balafons." A kora is a type of harp, and a balafon is a xylophone. The song's lyrics were written by the nation's first president, Léopold Sédar Senghor, and the music is by Herbert Pepper. It was adopted as the national anthem in 1960.

French lyrics

Pincez tous vos koras,
Frappez les balafons.
Le lion rouge a rugi.
Le dompteur de la brousse
D'un bond s'est élancé,
Dissipant les ténèbres.
Soleil sur nos terreurs,
Soleil sur notre espoir.
Debout, frères,
Voici l'Afrique rassemblée

Fibres de mon cœur vert.
Épaule contre épaule, mes plus que frères,
O Sénégalais, debout!
Unissons la mer et les sources,
Unissons la steppe et la forêt!
Salut Afrique mère.

English translation

Sound, all of you, your koras,
Beat the drums,
The red lion has roared,
The tamer of the bush
with one leap has rushed forward
Scattering the gloom.
Light on our terrors,
Light on our hopes.
Arise, brothers,
Africa behold united!

Fibers of my green heart.
Shoulder to shoulder,
O people of Senegal, more than brothers to me, arise!
Unite the sea and the springs,
Unite the steppe and the forest!
Hail, mother Africa.

CHAPTER 6

Up and Coming

Senegal has one of the fastest growing economies in the world. A development plan adopted by the government is helping with this progress. The plan includes investing in modernizing agriculture and industry, and improving roads and railways that deliver goods to markets and shipping ports. Tourism is also a large part of the development plan.

Senegal has become one of West Africa's major centers of trade and commerce. It has joined the African Continental Free Trade Area, a union of forty-four African countries that have agreed to trade goods and services with limited taxes and duties.

Despite the promise of economic advancement, Senegal still grapples with poverty and unemployment, especially among young people.

Opposite: **Fishers unload and sell their catch on the beach in Dakar.**

Working Overseas

Jobs can be scarce in Senegal. Many people must leave the country to find work. The most common destinations for Senegalese migrants are Spain, France, and Italy. It is estimated that 640,000 Senegalese work in Europe and the United States. They send home much of the money they earn to help support their families. Nearly one-tenth of the income in Senegal, more than $1 billion annually, comes from migrants who have left the country to work overseas.

Thousands of Senegalese immigrants live in New York City.

Agriculture

More than 70 percent of Senegalese workers are engaged in agriculture. Most farmers practice subsistence farming, which is growing food for family, community, and local markets. Farms are small, and most are owned in common with other members of the village. Every adult member of a village community has a piece of the farm. They help each other plant and harvest. Their tools are simple—hoes, shovels, and horse-drawn wagons and plows. Farmers rely on rivers or rain to supply water for their crops. They grow onions, carrots, millet, potatoes, eggplants, tomatoes, lettuce, tamarind, guava, and melons. Most people also keep chickens for eggs and meat.

Livestock rearing is another important part of rural agriculture. Herders raise cattle, goats, donkeys, and horses. In fertile river valleys, Senegalese raise their livestock near villages.

But in the Sahel and the savanna, herders are nomadic. They move about, guiding their livestock to grazing lands and water sources. In some areas, water is pumped from deep wells for animals. Sometimes as many as twenty thousand animals use the pumping stations each day. The livestock supplies villages and local markets with dairy products such as milk and soft cheese, which are important to the people's diets.

Cash crops, particularly peanuts, are a major part of Senegal's economy. Peanuts are grown in an area known as the peanut basin, which lies along the Senegal River outside of Dakar. Years of growing a single crop has depleted the nutrients in the soil in this area. Peanuts are also very dependent on rainfall, and Senegal has undergone several droughts in recent years. Efforts are being made to improve soils and develop a steady water supply. The Diama Dam, in northwest Senegal, was built to provide irrigation during droughts.

A truck in Senegal is piled high with bags of peanuts.

Other important cash crops include cotton, palm oil, cashews, and gum arabic. Senegal exports more than 25,000 tons of cotton each year. African oil palms are grown in the southern forests of the Casamance region. The palm oil collected from the fruit is used in making soap, cosmetics, candles, and biofuels. The palm kernel oil is used in making margarine, ice cream, cookies, bread, and medicines. Cashews, coconuts, and Brazil nuts are also farmed in the Casamance region. Gum arabic, a sap collected from acacia trees in the Sahel, is used for making many things, including glue, paint, cosmetics, chewing gum, and lotions.

What Senegal Grows, Makes, and Mines

Agriculture (2016)

Rice	885,284 metric tons
Peanuts	719,000 metric tons
Sugarcane	696,992 metric tons

Manufacturing (2016, value in exports)

Refined oil	$374 million
Chemical products	$337 million
Cement	$220 million

Mining

Gold (2017)	11,670 kilograms
Salt (2013)	240,000 metric tons

Fishing and Forestry

Fish is a key ingredient in the Senegalese diet. Some fishers ply the waters in pirogues, a traditional boat carved from a single tree trunk. Pirogues are the only way to navigate the rivers, where many places are shallow and narrow. A number of coastal fishers, based mainly out of Saint-Louis, use larger motorboats or small trawlers. The saltwater fishing industry has faced trouble in recent years from foreign fishing boats. They have overfished Senegal's fishing grounds. The government is taking measures to limit the number of licenses for foreign fishing operations.

A woman crushes palm nuts to make palm oil.

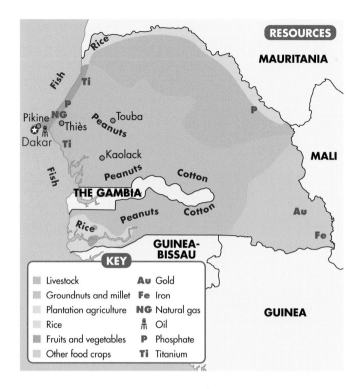

MAURITANIA

MALI

THE GAMBIA

GUINEA-BISSAU

GUINEA

KEY

Livestock	**Au** Gold
Groundnuts and millet	**Fe** Iron
Plantation agriculture	**NG** Natural gas
Rice	**⚒** Oil
Fruits and vegetables	**P** Phosphate
Other food crops	**Ti** Titanium

Senegal's forests are also in jeopardy. Trees are being logged for use in construction and furniture making, as well as for fuel and export. The practice is not sustainable since more trees are being logged than are being replanted. The rain forest region in the south is home to many prized hardwoods, such as teak and mahogany. Teak is a precious wood used in manufacturing garden furniture and boat decks. Mahogany is also prized for furniture making. The logging industry is small, but many hardwoods are logged illegally and smuggled out of the country. The government of Senegal is stepping up enforcement to stop illegal logging.

Mining and Manufacturing

Senegal's mineral resources include phosphate, gold, salt, natural gas, limestone, basalt, and petroleum. The chief exports are phosphates for making fertilizer, and limestone for making concrete. Senegal also has a wealth of untapped mining resources. Mines to extract iron ore, uranium, copper, zircon, and titanium are being developed. Major new deposits of oil and natural gas fields have been discovered off Senegal's coast.

Senegal's largest manufacturing industry is food processing. Food processing includes cleaning and freezing fish; shelling, roasting, and packaging peanuts and tree nuts; milling flour; and refining sugar. Agricultural products that are not food are also processed. Shea butter and palm oil are turned into lotions, and cotton is woven into cloth.

In major cities, factories manufacture shoes, clothing, and furniture. Many kinds of goods are produced in small workshops, including blown glass, musical instruments, textiles, pottery, and jewelry.

Senegalese work among piles of salt along the shores of Lac Rose. They are collecting and bagging the salt for export.

Services

The service industry makes up the largest part of the economy of Senegal. Service workers are people who do jobs for others, such as teachers, health care workers, restaurant and hotel workers, tour guides, taxi drivers, bankers, construction workers, and firefighters. Cities, especially Dakar and Saint-Louis, are expanding and creating more service jobs. Tourism is rapidly expanding in Senegal. Europeans, especially the French, travel there for the beaches, nightlife, shopping, and outdoor excursions.

Communication

Senegalese citizens are well connected to each other. There are nearly as many cell phones in use as there are people. Satellites provide access to TV programming and the internet. Internet media includes newscasts from sources such as All Africa, Al Jazeera Africa, and the Senegal Post. The government broadcasts five television stations and a national radio network. Private broadcast companies provide television and radio programs.

Several newspapers are published in Dakar. The most widely read is *Le Soleil*. However, the literacy rate is low in Senegal, and most people get their news and entertainment through television, radio, and the internet.

Energy

Government officials and private businesses are getting serious about improving the country's energy needs. Although 90 percent of Senegalese living in urban areas have electricity,

Senegal's Currency

The currency of Senegal and seven other West African nations is the West African CFA franc. CFA stands for Communauté Financière Africaine (African Financial Community).

Each CFA franc is divided into 100 centimes. Coins come in denominations of 1, 5, 10, 25, 50, 100, 200, and 500 CFA francs. Banknotes come in denominations of 500, 1,000, 2,000, 5,000, and 10,000 CFA francs. The banknotes show images related to the economy on the front and animals on the back. For example, on the front of the 500 CFA franc note is an image of a bronze figure resembling a sawfish, which was once used to weigh gold. It represents prosperity. Alongside the sawfish is an image of a hand and a computer tablet superimposed over a map of Africa. It symbolizes modernization and African unity. On the reverse side is a picture of two hippopotamuses, which represent Africa's natural wealth.

The CFA franc has been used in West Africa since 1945.

Senegal recently adopted an eCurrency, which makes bank transactions easier. In 2018, $1 equaled 559 West African CFA francs.

only about 30 percent in rural areas do. Electricity is mainly produced by coal-burning power plants.

Renewable energy is developing. Three out of the four dams along the Senegal River produce electricity. Wind power plants are being considered off Senegal's breezy coastline. The government is working on a project to provide fourteen thousand rural villages with solar power. In the northern Sahel, near the town of Bokhol, is a site containing seventy-five thousand solar panels, one of the largest solar plants in West Africa.

CHAPTER 7

One People, One Goal

THE PEOPLE OF SENEGAL ARE ETHNICALLY DIVERSE, but they share a common allegiance to their country. There may be occasional social conflicts, but people show respect for each other's ethnic heritages and cultural differences. The country's official motto is "One People, One Goal, One Faith."

Opposite: **A woman from northern Senegal carries her child on her back. On average, women in Senegal have five children.**

Wolof People

The largest ethnic group by far is the Wolof. More than 40 percent of the population is of Wolof heritage. Much of their traditional land is centered on the peanut basin region. Their language is often the language of trade between villages, marketplaces, and even other ethnic groups.

Wolof people were the first in Senegal to interact with the French. They achieved wealth and power in the nineteenth

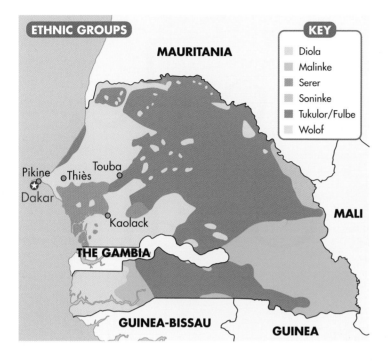

ETHNIC GROUPS

MAURITANIA

KEY
- Diola
- Malinke
- Serer
- Soninke
- Tukulor/Fulbe
- Wolof

Pikine
Thiès
Touba
Dakar
Kaolack

THE GAMBIA

MALI

GUINEA-BISSAU

GUINEA

Ethnic Groups

Wolof	41.6%
Tukulor/Fulbe	28.1%
Serer	15.3%
Malinke	5.4%
Diola	3.4%
Soninke	0.08%
Other (Other African ethnic groups, métis, French, Lebanese, Chinese, Vietnamese)	5.4%

century by trading goods and enslaved people to the French and helping produce peanuts and gum arabic. Many Wolof people moved to one of the four communes in Senegal, where they gained full rights as citizens of France.

Today, Wolof people live in both small villages and big cities. In the villages, most men are farmers, growing and selling cash crops. Women perform household tasks, raise children, and tend kitchen gardens. Many are skilled weavers.

In the cities, people of Wolof heritage have long been established in fields such as international trade, shipping, tourism, and the arts. Many Wolof people work in government and civil service. They are also known as style setters. Their clothing is fashionable, and their hairstyles are elaborate.

In the colonial era, many Wolof women married French colonists. Their children were known as *métis*, meaning "half." The métis formed their own society. They spoke French and Wolof and followed the social ways of the French as well as the Wolof. Many métis men and women were active in politics. Today, the largest métis communities are found in Saint-Louis and on Gorée Island.

People of the Futa Toro Valley

The Futa Toro valley along the Senegal River is the site of one of the most ancient settlements in Senegal. The two major groups that live in the valley are the Tukulor and the Fulbe. Members of these two groups have long intermarried, and much of their culture has blended. Together, the Tukulor and the Fulbe people make up about 28 percent of the population.

Many Wolof women supplement their family's income by weaving and selling baskets.

Among the Tukulor, people fish, farm millet and sorghum to sell, and tend kitchen gardens for their own food. Some are craftspeople. The Tukulor people have a strict social structure. Property is owned by men and is passed down through the males in the family. Households are generally made up of a father, sons, their wives, and grandchildren. Tukulor men often have more than one wife. This pattern may be changing, however. Today, about 20 percent of young men have a single wife. Many young people are leaving village farms and moving to cities to earn a living.

A Fulbe woman collects milk from her family's cows.

Pulaaku

Pulaaku is the Fulbe and Tukulor moral code of conduct. Fulbe and Tukulor people are proud and hardworking. They teach their beliefs to children at a young age. There are three pillars of Pulaaku: *munyal* (patience and self-control); *semteende* (modesty, respect); and *hakkille* (wisdom).

An elderly Fulbe man. In Senegal, people live an average of sixty-seven years.

The Fulbe people are traditionally nomadic herders. The Fulbe first came to Senegal hundreds of years ago from North Africa. They established themselves in the Futa Toro valley and lived among the Tukulor. Many still work as nomadic herders and traders. The Fulbe people primarily raise cattle. The more cattle a Fulbe man owns, the higher his status in society.

The Fulbe people are known for their appreciation of beauty. They wear colorful clothing and heavy jewelry. Men and women have tattoos, and women decorate their faces and bodies with henna dye. Being brave is an important quality in men. In their games, young boys are encouraged to play rough and be fearless.

Serer, Malinke, Diola, Soninke

The Serer people, who make up about 15 percent of the population, are closely related to the Wolof. Their historic homelands are along the Saloum and Gambia River deltas and along the coast south of Dakar. Many Serer people follow their traditional occupations of fishing and boatbuilding.

About 5 percent of Senegalese are Malinke. Originally from the Mali Empire, they moved across Senegal in search of better farmlands. They settled near the Gambia River and in the

Diola women dance at a ceremony.

Casamance region. Malinke men hunt, fish, farm, and herd animals. Women help plant and harvest and care for children and the home. The Malinke people live in close villages. Their thatched-roof homes are built around a central square.

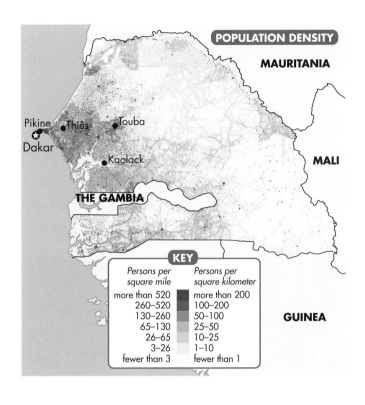

The Diola people live in the Casamance region. They were the last group to be taken over by the French. Today, many Diola are planters who operate large-scale farms growing peanuts, oil palms, and rice. Historically, their wealth was measured in how much rice a farmer had.

The Soninke people once ruled the Empire of Ghana. Some Soninke migrated to Senegal and established villages in Bakel, a town along the Senegal River. There, they mainly farm millet, although many young people have moved to Dakar to study or work.

Other Groups

Various other ethnic groups combine to make up about 5 percent of Senegal's population. Many belong to small African ethnic groups, such as the Bambara from Mali and the Kolda from Casamance. The Bassari live in an isolated area near Niokolo-Koba National Park. The Lebu people were originally

Population of Major Cities	
Dakar	2,476,400
Pikine	874,062
Touba	529,176
Thiès	317,763
Kaolack	233,708

residents of Cap Vert. Today, they continue to live in their traditional homeland at the tip of Cap Vert and mostly fish for a living.

Some people who live in Senegal have roots in other parts of the world. Thousands of French citizens live in Senegal. Several generations of Lebanese, many of whom own retail stores and factories, immigrated to Senegal to escape war in their home country. Recently, Chinese and Vietnamese workers and businesspeople have immigrated to Senegal.

A Chinese cloth merchant bargains with customers at his shop in Dakar. Most Chinese in Senegal are shopkeepers.

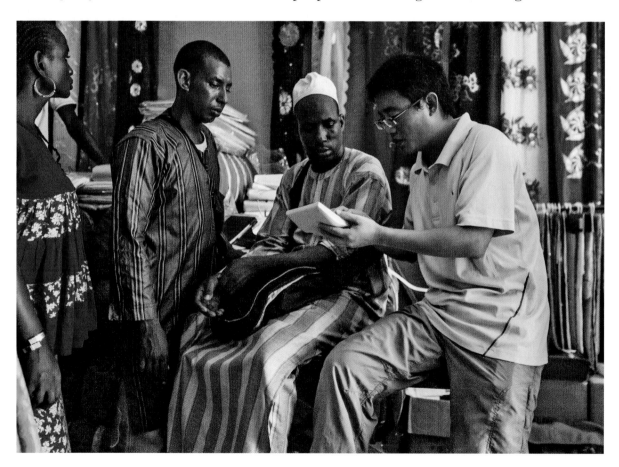

Women attend a literacy class where they learn to read Wolof.

Languages of Senegal

Wolof and French are the most common languages spoken in Senegal. Here are a few phrases:

English	Wolof	French
How are you? (formal)	*Na nga def?*	*Comment allez-vous?*
I am fine, and you?	*Jàmm rekk. Yow nag?*	*Je vais bien et vous?*
How are you? (to a friend)	*Yaa ngi noos?*	*Comment ça va?*
Please	*Baal ma*	*S'il vous plait*
Thank you	*Jërëjëf*	*Merci*

Language

French is the official language of Senegal, but most Senegalese do not speak it. Most ethnic groups have their own language, and the government recognizes twenty languages other than

Only about 60 percent of children complete primary school. Many must leave school to help their families.

French. Many of these languages fall into two language families. The Atlantic family is spoken in the west by the Wolof, Serer, Fulbe, Tukulor, and Diola. The eastern languages are from the Mande language group. Speakers of a Mande language include the Bambara, Malinke, and Soninke.

The most common language is Wolof. Not only do members of the Wolof ethnic group speak it, but many other people speak it as a second language. Because of this, Senegalese of different ethnic groups often communicate in Wolof.

Education

Primary education is free to Senegalese children up to age sixteen. Children are required to attend school for six years, except in communities where parents want their children to attend Islamic schools. Children must pass an examination after six years of school to be able to study further. If success-ful, children move on to middle school. After passing another examination after two years, students can attend high school. Students who do not or are unable to finish high school but want to continue an education often become apprentices. Many cities also have private Catholic schools.

Both public and private schools are taught in French even though few Senegalese speak it. In 2018, ninety-eight schools began teaching elementary students in Wolof. People behind the program believe that students will learn more studying in the language they speak at home.

About 20 percent of Senegalese children attend Catholic school, even though the vast majority of the population is Muslim.

The literacy rate is low in Senegal. Only an estimated 58 percent of people over age fifteen can read and write. In rural areas, children are often called upon to work in the fields. Some children also leave school because they cannot afford to buy uniforms, books, and school supplies.

Senegal has several colleges. The largest is Cheikh Anta Diop University in Dakar, which was established as a medical school in 1918. Today, sixty thousand students attend the school, studying math, science, architecture, literature, engineering, finance, and medicine.

The library at Cheikh Anta Diop University is a striking modern building.

Young talibés head out into the street to beg.

The Plight of the Talibés

Many devout parents in Senegal choose to send their sons to an Islamic school to study the Qur'an, the Islamic holy book. Most of these schools, called *daaras*, are found in Dakar and other large cities. They are run by holy men called marabouts. In the daaras, the students, called *talibés*, study only the Qur'an.

Marabouts send the talibés into the streets to beg for money and food. In Dakar, thousands of talibés fill the streets. Begging is an old tradition, and many people believe that begging teaches the children humility. In the evening, talibés give the money and any gifts people give them to the marabout.

Many talibés are not treated well. The government is increasing regulations on these schools. In some places, students have been removed from the schools and sent home to their parents.

For many people in Senegal, the plight of the talibés is a clash between the old ways and the modern world.

CHAPTER 8

Harmony and Faith

NEARLY ALL SENEGALESE PRACTICE ISLAM. MANY also believe in Sufism, a mystical form of the faith. Some Senegalese, including French, Lebanese, and Vietnamese, practice Christianity. Most Christians in Senegal belong to the Roman Catholic faith.

Although most Senegalese are Muslim, ancient cultural traditions influence people's faith. In some isolated villages, people continue to practice ancient religions. Senegal has no official religion, and the constitution promises everyone the freedom to practice the faith of their choice.

Opposite: **A worshipper carries his shoes through the Great Mosque in Touba. Everyone must remove their shoes before entering a mosque.**

Animism

Before Islam arrived in what is now Senegal, most people practiced a form of animism. Animism is the belief that spirits exist in all things, including animals, plants, rocks, water,

earth, and sky. Many ethnic groups in Senegal also traditionally believed in a single creator. For example, the Fulbe people believed in Geno, the eternal creator, while the Serer believed in one all-powerful god called Roog.

Islam

Muslims believe that God, "Allah" in the Arabic language, delivered his teachings in messages to a prophet named Muhammad. These messages are said to have been collected and put in a book known as the Qur'an.

Berber traders from North Africa brought the Muslim religion to Senegal. In the eleventh century, the Tukulor people became the first in Senegal to adopt Islam. They spread the belief to other groups. In the fifteenth century, the Wolof people adopted Islam, spreading the faith still wider across Senegal.

Many marabouts mix Islam and traditional African religions, sometimes performing the role of a fortune-teller.

The Five Pillars of Islam

Muslims practice a set of duties called the Five Pillars of Islam. They are:

1. To believe that there is one God, and that Muhammad is the messenger of God.
2. To pray five times a day.
3. To give to charity.
4. To fast from sunrise to sunset for the holy month of Ramadan (the ninth month of the Islamic calendar).
5. To make a pilgrimage, if one is able, to the holy city of Mecca, Saudi Arabia, the birthplace of Muhammad.

Muslims sometimes use prayer beads to keep track of short prayers that they repeat many times.

In the early centuries of Islam in Senegal, groups of religious families immigrated from the east. The elders of the groups were spiritual leaders, called marabouts. Some ethnic leaders aligned themselves with the marabouts and gave them land to start their own villages. Many people moved into the marabouts' villages, giving them more power. Today, these spiritual leaders, who can be men or women, remain at the heart of Muslim society in Senegal. They guide people in prayer and instruct the young in the Qur'an.

Marabouts sometimes blend the beliefs of traditional African religions with Islam. Historically, marabouts made amulets called *gris-gris* out of carved shell, wood, leather, or bone. People would wear the amulets to ward off evil and bring good fortune. In pre-Islamic times, holy men filled gris-gris with bits of bone or powders. Today, marabouts might make amulets and fill them with slips of paper inscribed with scriptures from the Qur'an. They also solve disputes, arrange marriages, and manage social and business relationships.

Amulets are often made of cowrie shells.

The Mosque of the Divinity sits right near the ocean in Dakar.

Places of Worship

Mosques are places of worship where Muslims pray. There are tens of thousands of mosques in Senegal. No village in Senegal is likely to be without a mosque or Islamic learning center.

Some of the oldest, constructed in the fifteenth century, are in Futa Toro. Most of those are made of mud brick and adobe. The structures are supported by pairs of wooden poles that protrude from the adobe walls. After the rainy season washes away the outer layers of mud, villagers use the poles as scaffolding to apply fresh mud to the exterior walls. In their simplicity, the adobe mosques with mud minarets, arched walls, and domes are works of art.

Other mosques are among the grandest sights in Senegal. The Great Mosque of Touba, one of the largest in all of Africa, is built of pink marble from Italy. The exterior of the Grand Mosque of Dakar is finished in traditional blue Moroccan tiles. Its minaret—a tower attached to a mosque—houses eight floors of classrooms.

Sufism

Sufism is a mystical, emotional way of practicing the Muslim faith. In Senegal, most Muslims are Sufis. Sufis disregard wealth and material possessions. They are humble, selfless, and live simply. "Little sleep, little talk, little food" is a code they live by. Sufi leaders use music, movement, and poetry to pray. In some ceremonies, they may enter into a religious trance. Followers believe Sufi spiritual guides are saintlike.

In the twelfth century, Sufi leaders created the Sufi Paths, or Brotherhoods. There are four Brotherhoods in Senegal: Xaadir, Tijaniyyah, Layene, and Mouride. Of them, the

A member of the Mouride Brotherhood prays at the tomb of Sheikh Amadou Bamba in Touba.

Pilgrims line up to enter the Great Mosque of Touba during the Grand Magal.

Grand Magal

Sheikh Amadou Bamba is buried in the village of Touba. In 1963, Senegal's largest mosque, the Great Mosque of Touba, was completed next to his tomb. Touba is Senegal's holiest site. Visitors constantly flow into the mosque to pray. One of the biggest celebrations in all of Islam is the Grand Magal of Touba, which honors the life of Sheikh Bamba. More than one million Muslims from throughout West Africa come for the Grand Magal festival. They meet with marabouts and listen to Sheikh Bamba's poetry read and sung aloud.

Mourides are by far the most powerful and influential, both religiously and politically.

The Mouride Brotherhood was founded in the city of Touba in 1883 by Sheikh Amadou Bamba, a Sufi marabout and mystic. He wrote poetry emphasizing hard work, meditation, and prayer. During the French colonial period, the sheikh led a peaceful resistance and was exiled. After years

A Catholic priest baptizes a Senegalese baby. About 3 percent of Senegalese are Catholic.

of banishment, the French asked him to return to help enlist his followers into the army during World War I. He was later awarded the French Legion of Honor medal, which is the country's highest honor. Today, about four million Senegalese belong to the Mouride Brotherhood.

Religion in Senegal (2016)	
Islam	96.1%
Christian (mostly Roman Catholic)	3.6%
Animist	0.3%

Religious Tolerance

In many parts of the world religious conflict is common, and West Africa is no exception. Yet Senegal is unlike many of its neighbors. The country's first president, Léopold Senghor, was Christian, and he believed in religious freedom. As a result, people in Senegal celebrate each other's religious holidays and many Muslims attend Catholic private schools.

Examples of people sharing in each other's religion include Muslims giving Christmas gifts and decorating Christmas trees. Also, Christians celebrate the Muslim festival of Tabaski, which commemorates the Bible story about Abraham, a man willing to sacrifice his son to God. In the story, God, at the last moment, replaces the boy with a lamb. To celebrate, Muslim families slaughter a sheep or goat, enjoy a great feast, and give one-third of the meat to the poor. Everywhere in Dakar leading up to the festival, goats can be seen tied to the roofs of cars.

A Christmas nativity set for sale on Gorée Island

Harmony and Faith

CHAPTER 9

Color and Rhythm

THE ARTS OF SENEGAL ARE BOTH STRIKINGLY MODern and deeply traditional. Over centuries, the country's many ethnic groups have created a colorful mosaic of painting, sculpture, music, dance, fashion, storytelling, and crafts. Unique Senegalese musical styles, which blend the ancient and the new, have inspired musicians throughout the world. Senegalese artisans take traditional objects of everyday usefulness and create an array of decorative crafts.

Today's rich cultural life was helped by the support of the nation's first president, Léopold Senghor. A poet himself, he valued many different art forms and established museums, art schools, and cultural centers. More recently, President Macky Sall has followed Senghor's example and transformed a historic courthouse into a major art exhibition hall.

Opposite: **Drumming is often a central part of festivals in Senegal.**

Craft Traditions

The earliest art forms in Senegal were crafts such as weaving, basketmaking, pottery, jewelry making, and blacksmithing. Each ethnic community created its own style.

Traditionally, Wolof girls learned from their mothers, aunts, and grandmothers how to make coiled baskets using grass and palm fronds. In markets today, many Wolof weavers sell sturdy and decorative baskets made from colorful recycled plastic. The city of Thiès is known for the production of tapestries. The images woven are based on the paintings of modern Senegalese artists such as Ousmane Faye and Amadou Seck. Tapestries produced in Thiès are displayed in museums around the world.

A young Bedik woman in eastern Senegal wears elaborate jewelry.

The Meaning of Masks

As elsewhere throughout Africa, Senegalese groups have made masks as part of their spiritual life. The masks are carved from wood and decorated with shells, beads, paint, fabrics, grasses, or tree bark. The Fulbe people carve large wooden masks, some more than 5 feet (1.5 m) tall. The Diola carve animal masks that are said to have powers to change the future. Mask wearers embody the spirit of the mask as they wear them in ceremonies to pray for rain and for good harvests as well as to celebrate marriages, births, and coming-of-age events.

A Diola person wears a mask at a ceremony in Casamance.

The Fulbe people are known for their tradition of making jewelry out of gold, silver, iron, copper, and brass. They also fashion beads from glass, wood, bone, and stone. Historically a nomadic group, the Fulbe knew that one of the easiest means of transporting their wealth was to wear jewelry.

In most ethnic groups in Senegal, pottery is made by women. They dig clay, mainly during the rainy season, when the clay is black. The potters coil ropes of clay and stack them into shape. Pots are set in the sun to dry or fired in a pit fueled by millet husks, wood, and cow dung. Some pots are burnished with iron oxide and others are decorated with symmetrical patterns.

Art

Glass paintings and other art are on display at a gallery in Dakar.

A time-honored Senegalese art form is glass painting. In this art form an image's finest details must be painted first and the background last. Common themes are village life and Qur'anic stories. Some Senegalese artists paint with colored sand, which they glue to wood with gum arabic.

Huge graffiti murals cover many walls on the streets of Dakar.

Graffiti Art

Graffiti is a vital and significant art form in Senegal. It has its own festival, a ten-day international arts event known as Festigraff. Displayed on fences, walls, and bridges, graffiti is true public art. Much Senegalese graffiti art touches on society's problems.

Dieynaba Sidibe is Senegal's first major woman graffiti artist. She focuses on women's roles in society and how women deserve equal pay and greater respect. Sidibe has explained, "There are so many families in Senegal whose mothers keep them together. These women wake up at four in the morning to go to the market and sell fish, and with the money they make they buy food and make a meal. The young men are asleep that whole time, so they wake up and find food. They have no idea what their mothers went through to get that meal on the table."

Contemporary Senegalese artists are often inspired by styles and subjects of the past, yet they make art that is dramatic and new. The father of contemporary Senegalese art was an abstract painter named Souleymane Keita. He sometimes represented ideas closely tied to his homeland, as in a series of paintings about Gorée Island. Viyé Diba is known for paintings and other works that use trash and other objects to express the need for social and economic change. Mamady Seydi makes large sculptures based on Senegalese folktales. Ousmane Sow was a sculptor who used bronze, clay, wood, stone, fabric, and rubber to create life-sized figures of warriors, wrestlers, and supernatural creatures. His work is shown in museums and galleries around the world.

Senegalese art is highly regarded internationally. Every two years, the Dak'Art Biennale in Dakar features more than two hundred exhibits of important contemporary African art.

Ousmane Sow's powerful sculptures earned him acclaim around the world.

The IFAN Museum

The Fundamental Institute of Black Africa (IFAN) in Dakar is one of the oldest African art museums in West Africa. The museum features thousands of important artifacts from historic and ancient Senegal and elsewhere in West Africa. Displays include ancient weapons, carvings, fabrics, masks, drums, pots, jewelry, and farm tools. The museum also includes temporary exhibits of contemporary Senegalese art. It is one of the main exhibit halls for the Dak'Art Biennale.

UNIVERSITE DE DAKAR
I F A N
MUSEE DE DAKAR

IFAN was founded in 1938 to study the culture and history of the people of West Africa.

Music

Senegal is well known for its distinct and lively music. The sounds of contemporary Senegalese music are drawn from the voices and rhythms of traditional music. Most musical styles are based on drumming and singing. Early musicians in Senegal were griots who sang songs to teach and to entertain. They were accompanied by villagers who chanted along and played drums, stringed instruments, and *shekeres*, dried gourds wrapped in beads.

Traditional music in Senegal features a variety of drums. The *nder* drum plays the lead sound. The *sabar* is the rhythm drum and is the main drum used in festivals and joyous ceremonies such as weddings and baby-namings. The sabar is the base of the unique Senegalese music style known as *mbalax*, which means "rhythm" in Wolof. Many contemporary musicians have become famous around the world for their upbeat

Youssou N'Dour is renowned for his large vocal range.

mbalax music. They include Youssou N'Dour, Orchestra Baobab, Baaba Maal, and Pape Diouf.

Other instruments essential to the sounds of Senegal are the *tama*, also known as the talking drum because it sounds similar to a human voice; the *kora*, a twenty-one-stringed harp; the *balafon*, a type of xylophone; and the *halam*, a stringed instrument said to be the forerunner of the American banjo. Hundreds of years ago, the special sounds and styles of Senegalese music were brought to the Americas during the time of slavery. Senegalese music inspired Afro-Cuban pop, American blues, reggae, and jazz.

Senegalese hip-hop is a popular musical form today. Hip-hop has historical roots in a Senegalese music style called *tassu*. Traditional tassu is spoken word accompanied by women playing drums and shekeres.

Literature

In Senegal, literature was traditionally oral. Stories were passed down from generation to generation by griots. Even as Senegalese produce abundant novels, poetry, and drama, griots still perform in ceremonies throughout the country.

Senegalese president Léopold Senghor published his first book of poems after being released from a German prisoner-of-war camp in 1945. Mariama Bâ wrote novels about the struggles of African women and the need for improving their lives. She was published in English as well as French and won the Noma Award for Publishing in Africa. Ousmane Sembène is likely the most widely read Senegalese author. His most

Fatou Diome's novel *The Belly of the Atlantic* was a best seller in France and was translated into several other languages, including English.

Color and Rhythm

famous book, *God's Bits of Wood*, tells the history of a railway strike against the French in colonial Senegal. Fatou Diome is a younger writer. Her first book, *The Belly of the Atlantic*, is about coming-of-age in modern Senegal.

Sports

Senegalese love lively, competitive sports. Throughout Senegal, young people can often be seen doing acrobatics or playing basketball or soccer. In 2016, Fatma Samba Diouf Samoura became secretary general of FIFA, the organization in charge of soccer's international tournaments, making her the first woman to run one of sports' most powerful organi-

Young men play soccer in a square on Gorée Island.

zations. She believes playing soccer erases conflicts about religion, gender, and race. Senegal's men's national team is nicknamed the Lions of Teranga. *Teranga* is a term for community and sharing.

Senegal's most popular sport is a wrestling event called *laamb*. Traditionally, after harvest time, villages would stage wrestling matches. Young men would take part to prove their intelligence and strength in the hopes of gaining respect and attracting a wife. Today, laamb is played on a large scale, and top wrestlers can become wealthy. Matches are played at major celebrations such as Independence Day. In Dakar, thousands of cheering fans pack into the wrestling stadium. Laamb matches are short—no more than fifteen minutes. Competitors use wrestling, judo, and boxing moves. Senegal also has a tradition of women wrestling, especially in the Casamance region. The nation's star woman wrestler, Isabelle Sambou, placed fifth in the 2012 Olympics.

Laamb has become the most popular sport in Senegal. Top matches are held in large arenas and are broadcast on television.

CHAPTER 10

Teranga

I N SENEGAL, *teranga* IS THE FOUNDATION OF HOME AND community life, the most important value among Senegalese people. Teranga is the belief that it is not what a person has that makes him or her wealthy, but how much a person gives to others. To practice teranga is to treat each other with kindness and generosity and to care for guests and strangers as if they were family.

Opposite: **Boys swing from a fishing boat on the beach in Dakar.**

Family and Community

Family is the center of Senegalese society. Families are large, with an average of about five children. Many Senegalese live in the same house or compound with grandparents, aunts, uncles, nieces, and nephews. Parents welcome each child with a grand celebration called *ngente,* an Islamic naming ceremony. Family, friends, and neighbors gather for a feast.

The mother prepares the food while the father consults with an imam or marabout about selecting a name. Babies are given the name of someone in the family or community. People consider it an honor to have a newborn named after them. They will play a special role throughout their namesake's life.

Family members have obligations to one another. The most important responsibility for children is showing respect for others. As a child grows, parents take on different responsibilities. Up to age seven, young children are allowed to play and run about. They are not yet expected to work. From age seven to thirteen, the children are taught to help with household chores, do their homework, and watch out for younger siblings. Mothers

A Bedik village in eastern Senegal is made up of round, thatched houses.

are expected to sacrifice for their children and build the children's character. Fathers are responsible for earning money to pay for food, shelter, and education. In the village, everyone takes on the responsibility of teaching children and correcting their mistakes, whether they are relatives or not. From age thirteen until twenty-one, children accept more responsibilities. Besides going to school, many also work and give money to their parents to help care for younger siblings. In their teen years, children need parents and mentors, such as close friends, aunts, or uncles, to teach them about the ways of the world and instill values such as honesty, teranga, *termonde* (compassion for the less fortunate), and *soutoura* (keeping secrets).

City and Village

Most Senegalese people live in rural areas, although more people are moving to cities to study or find jobs. Cities are noisy, lively, and colorful. Buses and taxis are painted bright colors, and many people, especially women, wear colorful clothing. Dakar is crowded and bustling. Many of the city's neighborhoods are a mixture of apartments and well-tended homes. Many homes in the poorer neighborhoods do not have electricity or clean running water.

Villages have average populations of a few hundred to one thousand. Nearly all villages have a community center or gathering spot, a mosque, and a community well. Housing styles often vary according to the group. Some homes are round mud brick with conical thatched roofs, others are rectangular with cement walls and tin roofs.

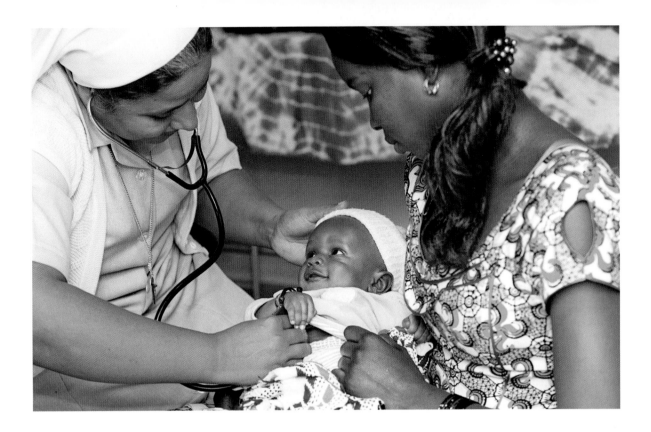

Forty-nine out of every one thousand children in Senegal die before the age of one. Foreign health organizations are working with the Senegalese to improve the health of children.

Health

The Senegalese people are at risk from a variety of dangerous diseases, many transmitted by insects. Malaria, carried by mosquitoes, is the best known, but mosquitoes can also carry dengue fever, yellow fever, and meningitis. Some black flies carry river blindness, while some tsetse flies can transmit sleeping sickness.

Combating serious disease in Senegal while also meeting everyday health care needs is a challenge. Nearly all of the country's hospitals are located in cities. Many villages do not have easy access to health clinics or pharmacies, and transportation can be a problem, especially in emergencies. Few roads are paved in the countryside, and during the rainy season many roads are impassable.

The government and foreign health organizations are working to expand the health care system. They have had some recent important successes. They have reduced cases of malaria by distributing mosquito nets, which prevent mosquitoes from biting people who are sleeping. Meanwhile, a new meningitis vaccine has nearly eliminated that disease.

Clothing

The people of Senegal wear a mixture of traditional and Western clothes. Especially in cities, men wear Western-style pants and shirts and women wear skirts or dresses. Only in Dakar do woman wear pants and men wear jeans. People also wear the traditional garment called the *boubou*. The boubou is made from soft cotton or silk, traditionally hand dyed, printed, and embroidered. It is a long robe, either flowing or narrow, and open at the sides. Underneath, women wrap a cloth around their bodies and men wear pants. Men who have made the hajj pilgrimage to Mecca wear a white boubou embroidered with gold thread. Women wear their hair in twists, braids, and elaborate updos. They also wear colorful patterned headscarves. People often dress in their best clothes on Fridays, the Muslim holy day of the week.

Food

Food in Senegal is a social experience. Many meals are served in a large bowl. Everyone eats from the bowl, usually by dipping with bread or simply using their hands. People rarely eat alone. When it is time for a meal, people stop what they are doing and gather together. Senegalese food is a flavorful mixture of fresh fruits, vegetables, rice, fish, meat, and spices. French colonists introduced breads and pastries. People drink coffee and juice, but mainly tea.

Thieboudienne is the national dish of Senegal. It is a combination of spicy stuffed fish with rice and vegetables, such as cassava, squash, and plantains. It is simmered and served in one bowl.

In Senegal, people eat using the right hand. The left hand is considered unclean.

Sweet Tea

Attaya is the Senegalese tea ceremony. It is celebrated in three rounds. In the first round, the tea is strong and bitter. Sugar and mint are added in the second round. The third round of tea is very sweet and has extra mint. The ceremony symbolizes the stages of friendship—the longer people are friends, the sweeter the friendship becomes.

Senegalese people usually drink green tea.

Fatayas are a favorite snack. They are fried pastries stuffed with onion, tomatoes, and fish and served with a spicy onion-tomato sauce called *kaani*. *Yassa* is a flavorful dish made from chicken marinated in lemon, spices, and onions.

Celebrations

Children are celebrated at their naming and coming-of-age celebrations. When it is time to marry, there are certain rituals to follow. The parents of a man interested in a woman must visit her family home. They bring money and kola nuts, which are a symbol of teranga. If the woman's parents approve, they accept the money and kola nuts and share the nuts with the

Games

Senegalese children play a variety of games that are similar to games familiar in the West. In the ocean, they play a form of tag called Mamadou Diop, which is similar to Marco Polo. Seynabou Dit is the name for the game Simon Says. All across Africa, children and adults play a board game commonly called mancala. In Senegal, it is known as *owaré*.

Ludo is a type of board game played in many African countries. It can be played by two or four people. Players move their four tokens from the start to the finish point according to the roll of the dice. The game board is a large cross with large squares at each corner and one center square. Small squares—the path—line the perimeters of the large squares. The goal is to get all tokens into the center square. If a player lands on a square where there is an opponent's token, the opponent's token must go back to start. When a player's token reaches the home stretch, the player must roll the exact number of spaces left to reach the center. Players can have all their tokens in play at the same time. The first to have all four tokens in the center wins.

neighbors as a wedding announcement. The future husband pays a dowry to his future wife's family. While some dowries can be expensive, such as a large gift of money or a house, many today are a token gift to express the union of two families. Many men, especially in the countryside, marry more than one wife. They must promise that each wife (no more than four) must be well provided for and treated equally.

Throughout the year, people celebrate holidays and festivals with feasting, music, drumming, dancing, and

Malinke people dance during a harvest celebration.

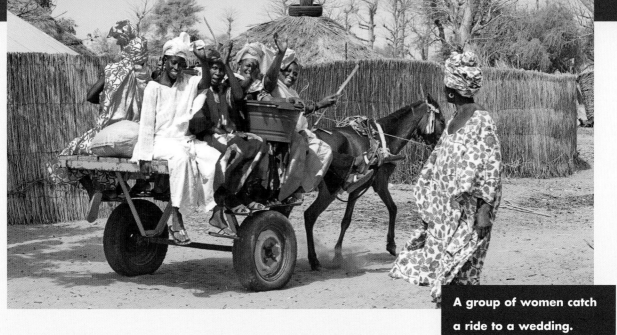

At the Wedding

In Senegal, young couples follow many different traditions in celebrating their marriage. Many Senegalese in Dakar and other large cities have what is called a "Western White" wedding. The bride wears a white gown and the groom wears a formal suit. Other people opt for a more traditional Senegalese ceremony. The bride and groom wear elaborate boubous. When the bride arrives at the wedding, she greets her female family members and friends who are wearing sad, serious faces to show their "sorrow" at losing her to her husband's family. The men stand to the side, often celebrating with songs and little dances.

Muslim marriages take place in the late afternoon at a mosque. Only the couple's families attend, symbolizing that marriage is also a union of families. After the ceremony, the groom gathers with his father, his uncles, and other male friends who give him marriage advice. Meanwhile, the bride and her female family members and friends leave for the wedding party. At the wedding party, people are dressed in their best clothes and dance throughout the evening. Often a griot is present to sing blessings for the couple.

storytelling. There are music festivals such as the Saint-Louis Jazz Festival; Rapandar, a four-day hip-hop and reggae festival; and the Abéné Festival, a ten-day drumming festival held in Casamance. Other special events include Kaay Fecc, a dance festival held in Dakar, and a boisterous carnival in Saint-Louis called Les Fanals, which features oversized parade floats.

The most important nonreligious holiday in Senegal is Independence Day, which is celebrated on April 4. Many parades are held throughout the country to mark the country's independence from France. Dakar has the largest parade, which features the military, police, and marching bands. Schools shut down for the holiday. All around Senegal people gather to celebrate their pride in their country and to enjoy the great company of family and friends.

Public Holidays

New Year	January 1
Easter	March or April
Independence Day	April 4
Whit Monday	April or May
Labor Day	May 1
Ascension Day	May
All Saints' Day	November 1
Christmas	December 25

Several Muslim holidays are also national holidays. Because the Islamic calendar is shorter than the Western calendar, the date of each holiday according to the Western calendar shifts from year to year.

Korité (End of Ramadan)
Tabaski (Feast of the Sacrifice)

Timeline

Senegalese History

200s BCE
People begin building stone circles along the Gambia River.

600s CE
What is now eastern Senegal becomes part of the Kingdom of Ghana.

11th century
The Tekrur kingdom becomes the first Senegalese group to adopt Islam.

1200s
Northern and eastern Senegal become part of the Mali Empire.

1360
The Wolof people become independent from the Mali Empire.

1375
Senegal becomes part of the Songhai Empire.

1445
Portuguese traders land on the Cap Vert Peninsula.

1536
Gorée Island becomes active in the Atlantic slave trade.

1659
The French found Saint-Louis at the mouth of the Senegal River.

Late 1850s
Umar Tal's Tukulor army fights the French.

1854
France appoints Louis Faidherbe governor of Senegal.

1885
European nations divide up Africa; France takes Senegal.

1914–1918
About 170,000 Senegalese fight f[or] the French during World War I.

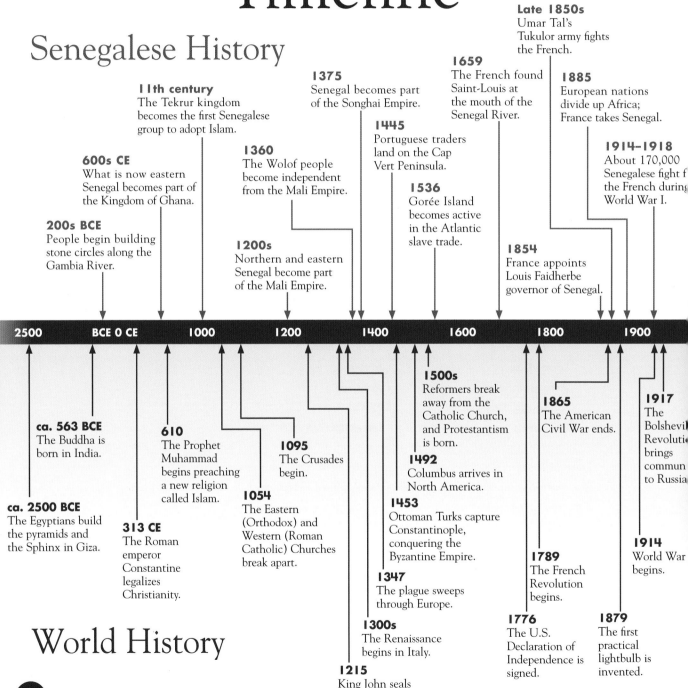

2500 | **BCE 0 CE** | **1000** | **1200** | **1400** | **1600** | **1800** | **1900**

World History

ca. 2500 BCE
The Egyptians build the pyramids and the Sphinx in Giza.

ca. 563 BCE
The Buddha is born in India.

313 CE
The Roman emperor Constantine legalizes Christianity.

610
The Prophet Muhammad begins preaching a new religion called Islam.

1054
The Eastern (Orthodox) and Western (Roman Catholic) Churches break apart.

1095
The Crusades begin.

1215
King John seals the Magna Carta.

1300s
The Renaissance begins in Italy.

1347
The plague sweeps through Europe.

1453
Ottoman Turks capture Constantinople, conquering the Byzantine Empire.

1492
Columbus arrives in North America.

1500s
Reformers break away from the Catholic Church, and Protestantism is born.

1776
The U.S. Declaration of Independence is signed.

1789
The French Revolution begins.

1865
The American Civil War ends.

1879
The first practical lightbulb is invented.

1914
World War begins.

1917
The Bolshevi[k] Revoluti[on] brings commun[ism] to Russia

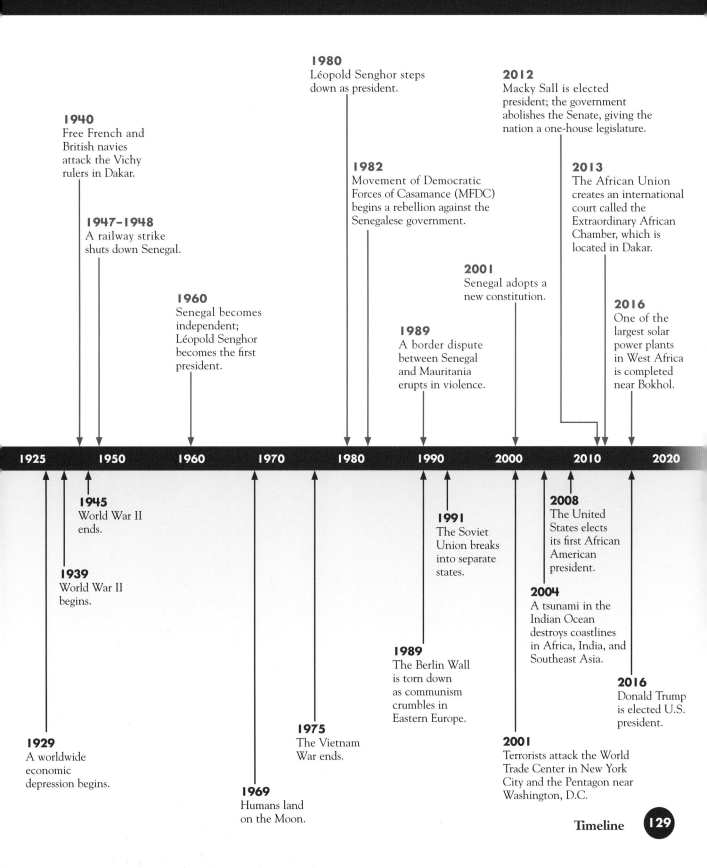

1940
Free French and
British navies
attack the Vichy
rulers in Dakar.

1947–1948
A railway strike
shuts down Senegal.

1960
Senegal becomes
independent;
Léopold Senghor
becomes the first
president.

1980
Léopold Senghor steps
down as president.

1982
Movement of Democratic
Forces of Casamance (MFDC)
begins a rebellion against the
Senegalese government.

2001
Senegal adopts a
new constitution.

1989
A border dispute
between Senegal
and Mauritania
erupts in violence.

2012
Macky Sall is elected
president; the government
abolishes the Senate, giving the
nation a one-house legislature.

2013
The African Union
creates an international
court called the
Extraordinary African
Chamber, which is
located in Dakar.

2016
One of the
largest solar
power plants
in West Africa
is completed
near Bokhol.

| 1925 | 1950 | 1960 | 1970 | 1980 | 1990 | 2000 | 2010 | 2020 |

1929
A worldwide
economic
depression begins.

1939
World War II
begins.

1945
World War II
ends.

1969
Humans land
on the Moon.

1975
The Vietnam
War ends.

1989
The Berlin Wall
is torn down
as communism
crumbles in
Eastern Europe.

1991
The Soviet
Union breaks
into separate
states.

2001
Terrorists attack the World
Trade Center in New York
City and the Pentagon near
Washington, D.C.

2004
A tsunami in the
Indian Ocean
destroys coastlines
in Africa, India, and
Southeast Asia.

2008
The United
States elects
its first African
American
president.

2016
Donald Trump
is elected U.S.
president.

Timeline 129

Fast Facts

Official name of the country:	Republic of Senegal
Capital:	Dakar
Official language:	French
Official religion:	None
Year of independence:	1960
National anthem:	"Pincez Tous vos Koras, Frappez les Balafons" ("Pluck Your Koras, Strike the Balafons")
Type of government:	Presidential republic
Head of state:	President
Head of government:	Prime minister

Left to right: **National flag, presidential guard**

Cap Vert peninsula

Area:	75,955 square miles (196,723 sq km)
Latitude & longitude of country:	14°0' N, 14°0' W
Bordering countries:	Mauritania to the north, Mali to the east, Guinea to southeast, Guinea-Bissau to the southwest, The Gambia is completely surrounded by Senegal in the south.
Length of coastline:	330 miles (531 km)
Highest elevation:	Near Népen Diakha, 1,906 feet (581 m) above sea level
Lowest elevation:	Sea level along the Atlantic Ocean
Longest river:	Senegal River, about 2,500 miles (4,000 km)
Average high temperature:	In Dakar, 77°F (25°C) in February, 87°F (31°C) in August
Average low temperature:	In Dakar, 64°F (18°C) in February, 78°F (26°C) in August
Average ocean temperature:	83°F (28°C) in August; 69°F (21°C) in February
Average annual precipitation:	13 inches (33 cm) in the north; 61 inches (155 cm) in the southwest

National population (2018 est.):	16,294,270	
Population of major cities:	Dakar	2,476,400
	Pikine	874,062
	Touba	529,176
	Thiès	317,763
	Kaolack	233,708

Landmarks:
▶ *African Renaissance Monument*, Dakar

▶ *Gorée Island Historical Museum*, Gorée Island

▶ *Great Mosque of Touba*, Touba

▶ *Niokolo-Koba National Park*, Kédougou Department

▶ *Saint-Louis colonial capital*

Economy: Seventy percent of workers in Senegal are employed in agriculture. Farmers work on subsistence and on commercial plantations producing peanuts, palm oil, and other cash crops. Senegalese farmers also raise goats, sheep, and cattle. Senegal mines produce phosphates, salt, gold, and other minerals. Both freshwater and saltwater fishing are important to the economy. Tourism is a growing industry in Senegal.

Currency: The West African CFA franc. CFA stands for Communauté Financière Africaine (African Financial Community). In 2018, $1 equaled 559 West African CFA francs.

System of weights and measures: Metric system

Literacy rate: 58%

Local words and phrases:

How are you? (formal)	Wolof: *Na nga def?*
	French: *Comment allez-vous?*
I am fine, and you?	Wolof: *Jàmm rekk. Yow nag?*
	French: *Je vais bien et vous?*
How are you? (to a friend)	Wolof: *Yaa ngi noos?*
	French: *Comment ça va?*
Please	Wolof: *Baal ma*
	French: *S'il vous plait*
Thank you	Wolof: *Jërëjëf*
	French: *Merci*

Prominent Senegalese:

Mariama Bâ *Novelist*	(1929–1981)
Sheikh Amadou Bamba *Sufi religious leader*	(1853–1927)
Youssou N'Dour *Musician*	(1959–)
Fatma Samba Diouf Samoura *First female secretary general of FIFA*	(1962–)
Léopold Senghor *First president*	(1906–2001)
Ousmane Sow *Sculptor*	(1935–2016)

Clockwise from top: **Currency, Youssou N'Dour, schoolchildren**

To Find Out More

Books

- Appiah, Kwame Anthony, and Henry Louis Gates, Jr., eds. *Encyclopedia of Africa*. New York: Oxford University Press, 2010.

- Friedenthal, Lora. *Religions of Africa*. Philadelphia: Mason Crest, 2014.

- Hobbs, Annelise. *West Africa*. Broomall, PA: Mason Crest Publishers, 2017.

- Sheehan, Sean. *Ancient African Kingdoms*. New York: Gareth Stevens, 2011.

- Thiam, Pierre, and Jennifer Sit. *Senegal: Modern Senegalese Recipes from the Source to the Bowl*. New York: Lake Isle Press, 2015.

Music

- Maal, Baaba. *The Traveller*. London: Marathon Artists, 2016.

- N'Dour, Youssou. *Fatteliku*. London: Real World Productions, 2015.

- *The Rough Guide to the Music of Senegal*. London: World Music Network, 2013.

- *Teranga! Senegal*. London: Sterns Africa, 2012.

- Visit this Scholastic website for more information on Senegal:
  www.factsfornow.scholastic.com
  Enter the keyword **Senegal**

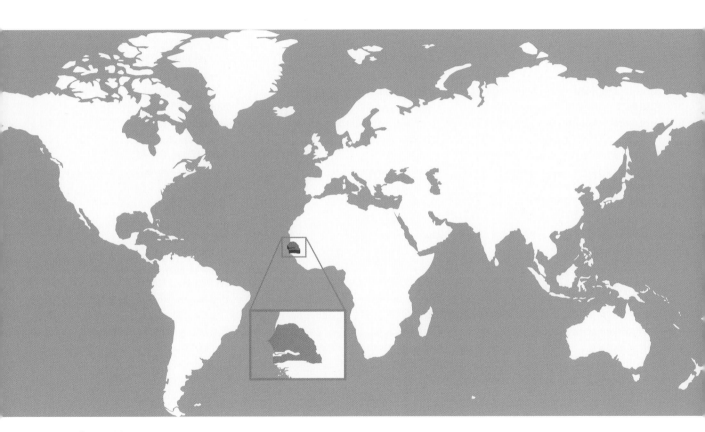

Location of Senegal

Index

Page numbers in *italics* indicate illustrations.

Meet the Author

RUTH BJORKLUND GREW UP IN RURAL NEW ENGLAND WHERE she enjoyed walks through the woods, rowing, kayaking, and sailing. After high school, she spent a year traveling around North America and eventually settled in Seattle, Washington, where she attended the University of Washington. She received a bachelor's degree in comparative literature and a master's degree in library and information science. She has been a children's and teen librarian and has written many books for young people on topics such as endangered animals, geography, theater and film, gun control, and immigration.

Today, Bjorklund lives on Bainbridge Island, a ferry ride away from Seattle. She continues to enjoy the outdoors, and she loves to travel. She has been to countries in South America, Asia, and Europe. In recent years, she has written several books about African countries, and she is captivated by the amazing variety of African cultures, art, music, fashion, wildlife, and landscapes.

Photo Credits